Praise for *The Ministry of Common Sense*

"As a business and culture transformation expert, Martin doesn't just chop off branches and leaves. He goes deep inside organizations to target the roots of inefficiency, impracticality, and general boneheadedness."
— Marshall Goldsmith, America's #1 Leadership Coach

"This gem is filled with useful (and fun) tips and tools that will help leaders build teams and organisations where common sense is the rule rather than the exception."
— Robert Sutton, Stanford professor and author of bestseller *The No Asshole Rule*

"Fun, fast-paced, and as actionable as it is insightful. Get ready to find out all the ways your organization can gain from better common sense. Highly recommended."
— Renée Mauborgne, INSEAD professor and co-author of the bestsellers *Blue Ocean Strategy* and *Blue Ocean Shift*

"*The Ministry of Common Sense* forces us all to take a hard look in the mirror if we want to take our businesses to the next level to win big - and do so by simply eliminating needless layers of corporate BRIGHT RED tape. Thanks for this book, Martin, because you have saved me from senseless meetings!"
— Tyra Banks, Supermodel turned Super Businesswoman

"Laughing aloud while reading a management book is not an everyday experience-and it happened to me dozens of times while reading *The Ministry of Common Sense*. Martin Lindstrom's 'common sense' approach is wise, humorous, and fundamentally practical. The book offers a path forward for engaging your employees in fixing broken systems to make work better and customers happier."
— Amy C. Edmondson, Harvard Business School professor and author of *The Fearless Organization*

"With wit and humor, Lindstrom argues that lack of empathy and blind acceptance of politics, technology, rules and regulations can strip us – and entire companies – of good judgment, damaging employee experience, culture, and customer satisfaction. If you are looking for a straight line to customer loyalty and financial success, check out *The Ministry of Common Sense*. It's a brilliant reminder that bringing humanity back to business just makes sense."

> – Liz Wiseman, bestselling author of *Multipliers* and *Rookie Smarts*

"A good-humored take on a serious subject--we are taking a daily bath in bureaucratic self sabotage. Plain-spoken and practical; a fun way to learn how to restore common sense to your organization"

> – Whitney Johnson, award-winning author of *Disrupt Yourself* and *Build an A Team*

"Bloated PowerPoints and endless meetings are just a few of the corporate practices that bog down the workplace in bureaucracy. The result is low morale, squandered productivity and poor decision-making. Thankfully, Martin Lindstrom offers specific solutions to restore common sense to organizations that sabotage their own success."

> – Carmine Gallo, communication advisor and bestselling author of *Talk Like TED*

"A must-read for anyone wishing to introduce more common sense practices and greater empathy in their workplace."

> – Keith Ferrazzi, Founder and Chairman of Ferrazzi Greenlight

"You will laugh, you will cry, and you will learn the power of common sense in this incredible gift of a book. Oh, and buy one for your boss too!"

> – Chester Elton, bestselling author of *The Carrot Principle, All In*, and *Leading with Gratitude*

"Lindstrom proves that, more often than not, the bigger your policy manual the smaller your organization's common sense. More importantly, he shows leaders at all levels how to reverse that alarming trend."

> – David Burkus, author of *Under New Management* and *Leading From Anywhere*

THE
MINISTRY
OF
COMMON SENSE

How to Eliminate
Bureaucratic Red Tape,
Bad Excuses,
and Corporate BS

MARTIN LINDSTROM

JOHN
MURRAY
LEARNING

First published in the United States in 2021 by Houghton
Mifflin Harcourt Publishing Company

First published in Great Britain by John Murray Learning in 2021
An imprint of John Murray Press
A division of Hodder & Stoughton Ltd,
An Hachette UK company

This paperback edition published in 2022

7

The acknowledgments on pp. 222–228 constitute
an extension of this copyright page.

Book design by Christopher Granniss

A CIP catalogue record for this title is available from the British Library

Paperback ISBN 978 1 529 33248 3
eBook ISBN 978 1 529 33249 0

Printed and bound in Great Britain by Clays Ltd, Elcograf S.p.A.

John Murray Press policy is to use papers that are natural, renewable
and recyclable products and made from wood grown in sustainable
forests. The logging and manufacturing processes are expected to
conform to the environmental regulations of the country of origin.

John Murray Press
Carmelite House
50 Victoria Embankment
London EC4Y 0DZ

www.johnmurraypress.co.uk

*For Gail Ursell, who came up with the idea,
and Bill Winters, who had the guts to run with it*

Common sense is the knack of seeing things as they are, and doing things as they ought to be done.

— Josh Billings

CONTENTS

CONTENTS

FOREWORD

Marshall Goldsmith

AS A BUSINESS EDUCATOR, COACH, AND AUTHOR, I typically work with successful people who want to get *better* at what they do. Sometimes that means counseling executives who have lost their "You Are Here" map. That blueprint could be internal — *Where am I going?* — or external — *How does what I do fit inside this organization?* Usually it's a mix of the two. The people I work with often come to understand that the skills that made them successful aren't always the same ones that can take them to the next level.

Why shouldn't this same confusion also affect organizations? Many companies have been doing what they do for so long, often so *well*, too, that they no longer question themselves. People *and* companies tend to be delusional about their strengths and weaknesses, focusing on the former and brushing aside the latter. (Usually this is obvious to outsiders, less so to anyone inside the company.) What many companies don't realize is that their success has come about not because of but in spite of various entrenched habits, behaviors, rules, policies, and cultures.

Martin Lindstrom has spent years as a pioneering global branding consultant. Thinkers50 has named him among the world's top fifty business leaders three years in a row. He's routinely behind so many dazzling innovations that sometimes it's a shock to realize they all originated in the same brain. More recently, Martin has repositioned his skills toward transforming global businesses and cultures from the inside out. Wherever he travels, he bangs up against the same problem again and again: the lack of common sense.

As humans, we suffer from the clash between who we think we are and who the rest of the world thinks we are. Spoiler: the world is usually right! I once defined "Mojo" (the title of one of my books) as "that positive spirit toward what we are doing now that starts from the inside and radiates to the outside" — one that leads to increased meaning, happiness, and employee engagement. By contrast, its dark twin — I call it "Nojo" — is "that *negative* spirit toward what we are doing now that starts from the inside and radiates to the outside." In the Nojo category we can now make room for the worldwide lack of common sense.

In this very funny, entertaining, informative book, Martin gives us numerous examples of where common sense has gone haywire in all kinds of organizations, whether it centers around dusty rules, endless meetings, poor customer experience, legal and compliance issues, you name it. But as a business and culture transformation expert, Martin doesn't just chop off branches and leaves. He goes deep inside organizations to target the roots of inefficiency, impracticality, and general boneheadedness. He also shows that a company's inner environment correlates with what consumers grapple with. The TV remote control you have no idea how to use and the corporate website that makes no sense link back to bottlenecks inside companies that management and employees are usually too inwardly focused to notice. Not least, where common sense is missing, Martin argues (convincingly too), so is empathy.

In my experience, when employees are doing what they choose to do, we typically see them as committed. If, on the other hand, they're doing what they *have* to do, we call them "compliant." Most companies have limited systems in place to honor what happens when a bad decision, or bad behavior, is averted. They focus on what they're *doing*, rather than on what they're *not* doing. In this book, Martin shows us what most companies *aren't* doing and *should* be doing—and offers a concrete solution to restore common sense and empathy to organizations of any shape or size.

I'm a longtime believer in 360-degree feedback as a way to help successful people figure out how to get better and improve their workplace relationships. In this book, Martin does his own high-scrutiny version of the 360. You'll be surprised. You'll be entertained. You'll be relieved. It's not just you! Finally, you'll be reminded that categories such as B2B or B2C aren't all that helpful, that in the end it all comes down to H2H, or human to human. It's common sense.

MARSHALL GOLDSMITH has been recognized by Thinkers50, *Fast Company, Inc.* magazine, and Global Gurus as the world's leading executive coach. He is the best-selling author of *What Got You Here Won't Get You There, Triggers,* and *Mojo.*

THE MINISTRY OF COMMON SENSE

INTRODUCTION

> Have you ever gotten locked out of your computer while
> you're at work? The good news, according to IT, is that
> support is available on their website — which you have
> no way to access since, well, you're locked out of your
> computer.

> Getting cc'd means you're part of the conversation,
> no one would think of leaving you out, and the team
> assumes you care about the solution to the problem
> you're being cc'd on. But at last count, there are 158
> emails in this thread, and you'd pay serious money to
> stop people from cc'ing you.

> You've submitted your travel itinerary to your department
> head but haven't heard back from her. Unfortunately, IT
> is set up in such a way that the travel form resets after
> twenty-four hours, which means you will have to fill out
> and submit your travel itinerary all over again.

> ➤ A nationwide chain of stores in the U.S. sells everything from washers and dryers to outdoor hammocks. So why does the company *also* have an internal policy requiring them to stock snow-removal equipment in their 100+ Florida locations, even though the last time it snowed in Florida was 1977?

TODAY, IT'S SAFE TO SAY we all confront one example after another that attests to the extreme want of common sense in our world. I certainly do. As a global consultant, I am ostensibly hired by organizations to create or fix brands. But nine times out of ten, I find myself serving as an organizational change agent, bringing to light and resolving corporate blindness and miscommunication, terrible customer service, products that make no sense or don't even work, packaging that sends us into a rage, and a general lack of intuitiveness both off- and online. I can confirm that the disappearance of common sense is at epidemic levels in companies not just in the United States but everywhere.

Last year when I was at the airport (I'm pretty much always at the airport), I splurged on a pair of new headphones. They were black, sound-isolating, Bluetooth-compatible, overpriced, and inconspicuous enough so that when I had them on I didn't look like a Teletubby. Collecting my receipt, I went on my way to my gate.

What I didn't know was that I'd be spending the next forty-five minutes trying and failing to extract my headphones from their package. The headphones were pinned down and held securely in place by a bubble of hard plastic resembling one-half of a Valkyrie's bra. The cord was trapped inside a separate plastic rectangle. No matter what I did and no matter what my angle of attack was, the plastic encasement simply wouldn't bend, dent, or move.

I tried wrenching the package apart with my fingers but stopped when my fingers started to hurt. I gnawed at it with my teeth but that only ended up hurting my teeth. I started banging the package repeatedly against one side of my seat like a piñata. Nothing worked.

This was now getting ridiculous, and crazy-making, and I had a flight to catch. I rummaged in my carry-on to see if I'd brought anything sharp with me, a house key or nail clippers, to somehow stab the plastic off, but I hadn't. Finally, I asked for help. "You don't have any scissors back there, do you?" I asked the ticket agent. Sorry, she didn't. "Or a knife?" No, and I could tell she would have preferred I not talk about scissors and knives at the boarding gate.

With not much time to go before my flight left, I raced back to the little kiosk where I'd bought the headphones. "Can you please help me?" I said to the cashier. Clearly it wasn't the first time something like this had come up. Removing a box cutter from his drawer, he sawed through the plastic for about a minute and finally handed over the headphones and the cord. "Do you want to take the container with you?" he asked. "No," I said. "I don't ever want to see the container ever again."

An experience like this is in almost delirious defiance of what could ever be defined as "common sense." To recap, I spent nearly $400 on a pair of headphones. For some reason, I left my chainsaw and other forestry equipment at home. Since I bought the headphones in an airport, obviously I'd forgotten to pack the ones I owned or, if it was an impulse purchase, which it was, I probably planned on wearing them during the flight to block out wailing babies or listen to music. But unless I'm missing something, how was I, or anyone, supposed to *open* them?

If it sounds like I've just cherry-picked an example to support the premise that the lack of common sense is pervasive or that my own experience in companies overlooks the sanity, practicality, discernment, and straightforwardness that define most global organizations, let me assure you that's wishful thinking.

Typically, a company hires me to identify the deeper purpose of a brand or to improve customer experience. I might be asked to create a new logo; redesign a website; brand a perfume, a beer, a wristwatch, or a retail environment. But in almost every case it soon becomes obvious that the *real* problem—the one responsible for lousy morale, lower-than-average productivity, frustrated customers, and an ongoing lack of innovation (despite leaders telling me how eager they are to "harness" or "unleash" new ideas across their organization, two words I've grown to hate)—is that companies have abandoned whatever common sense they once had in favor of systems and processes that a two-week-old golden retriever would find dumb. Either businesses never had much com-

> Companies are so entangled in their own internally generated issues, and further beset by reams of invisible red tape inside employees' heads, that they lose sight of their core purpose — and inevitably pay the price.

mon sense to begin with or they're not aware it's gone missing. This pervasive lack of common sense hampers the *real* business of companies — that is, serving their customers better than the competition and becoming more responsive, attentive, and attuned to their needs. Companies are so entangled in their own internally generated issues, and further beset by reams of invisible red tape inside employees' heads, that they lose sight of this core purpose — and inevitably pay the price.

It's a bigger problem than you can imagine. (Well, actually, you probably *can* imagine it.)

Two years ago, before COVID hit, I was hired by Swiss International Air Lines to reinvent the concept of economy class travel. At least that was the presenting problem. When I met with members of senior management, they clearly had certain aesthetic fixes in mind. Changing the welcome messages on the video screens, softening the glare of the reading lights, improving the snack selection. I told them that before I could even think about welcome messages, lighting, or snacks, I needed to figure out the *real* reasons why repeat passenger levels weren't as high as they once were and why the airliner ranked number eighteen in the industry for on-time arrivals. Over the next few months, I brought the cabin crew into passengers' homes so they could hear firsthand what it's like to be an airline passenger in the early twenty-first century. I convened ground staffers, pilots, and crew in one room so they could understand what their colleagues actually *did* for work. One word kept coming up to describe the experience of almost every flyer: "anxiety."

Anxiety while being in the air is only one part of it — that may be the most Arcadian part of the whole experience. There's anxiety about getting to the airport in a timely way.

There's anxiety about being in close proximity to strangers in airports, the TSA, fellow passengers, the airline crew — what if in addition to being terrorists, they're all silent carriers of COVID (or both)? Standing in line for a boarding pass, wondering if your suitcase or carry-on is oversized or over the weight limit. There's the security screening, the Transportation Security Administration guy reminding you for the one hundredth time to remove your laptop (*while* you're holding your laptop), emptying out your pockets, handing over your belt and shoes before someone asks you to wishbone your arms over your head as your belt-less pants inch farther and farther down your hips; another TSA employee scolds you for forgetting to remove the single Tic Tac that's buried in the lint of your shirt pocket. You've now cleared security, but there's more. There's anxiety about which zone or preferred category of customer gets to board the aircraft first (Jubilee Gold, Sapphire Silver, Sterling Platinum, Tequila Sunrise, or whatever), and guess what, you're in Zone 9, meaning you get to board simultaneously with the cargo, including a dead body, three angry German shepherds, and a Persian kitten named Mary Magdalene. Anxiety after the agent scans your ticket, when almost immediately you collide with a second long line waiting to advance through the aircraft doors. Anxiety as you clump past the business class passengers, wondering, *How did these turkeys end up here? They're not better than me. Where did I go wrong?* Anxiety as you try to find room for your carry-on in a tangle of arms, elbows, and mask-free passengers who've decided just to stand there in the aisle. Anxiety about your seatmates. About the takeoff. About turbulence and, of course, the plane crashing into the side of a mountain. Not to mention the possibility there's someone onboard who's completely off their rocker, the sort of person you read about in the *Daily Mail* under the headline, SHOCKING MOMENT WHEN AIRLINE PASSENGER . . .

There's anxiety around your arrival. Will there be snow or a heat wave? How long will it take to secure an Uber or a taxi? Is it rush hour? If you checked luggage, did the airline lose it, and if it didn't, will it be the last one to thump onto the carousel? On and on it goes.

More than welcome messages, reading lights, or snacks, the biggest issue around flying for most passengers is the mix of apprehension, uncontrollability, claustrophobia, and fear that make up the thing we call "anxiety."

I'm sorry, but seriously, is this news to anyone who's ever boarded an airplane? Isn't it just common sense? A few months later, a new department in the company was up and running. Focusing on ways to minimize anxiety for the average passenger, it also kept its eye on other places in the organization where common sense was conspicuously lacking. Soon the company began doing things differently.

Today, if you're a passenger taking a Swiss International flight from, say, Zurich to JFK, forty minutes before the plane lands, the pilot comes over the loudspeaker. In addition to giving gate numbers, the pilot then tells you how long the wait times are at customs and immigration and gives you a weather report and an estimate of how long it will take to walk from the gate to the luggage area (or to immigration) and for your taxi or car service to reach the city. The airline isn't responsible for any of these things and has no control over them — but you get off the plane knowing the airline takes your time considerations, your feelings, and your anxiety levels seriously.

There was another common-sense issue the airline hadn't

picked up on. Typically when you disembark from a plane, an orange-jacketed cleaning crew is waiting in the wings to board. They storm the aircraft, flipping up the armrests, vacuuming, scrubbing and wiping down surfaces, and bagging cans, wrappers, magazines, newspapers, and anything else passengers have left behind. They then make a concerted effort to push the armrests into their default positions. Why, though? A colleague of mine timed how long it took the average passenger to maneuver past a lowered armrest to get to the middle or window seat, versus when the armrest was raised. Two or three seconds. He did the math. There are 220 to 240 seats on an airbus. The cleaning crew raised and lowered every single armrest. It was the lowering part that took up valuable time. Why not keep the armrests upright, so that it's easier for passengers to board and slide across into their seats?

In less than a year, Swiss International Air Lines has become synonymous in customers' minds with timeliness, consideration, and empathy. Revenues are up, and so is the number of returning passengers. Department divisions and services that never saw the need to communicate are now working together pretty much seamlessly, and *Business Insider* recently named it the number two airline in Europe.

Fifty percent or so of all the people on earth work for some sort of organization. A business. A government agency. A school or college. A hospital. A bank or insurance firm. A research company. A media or pharmacological conglomerate. When I ask the people in charge how many common-sense issues there are in their organizations, most squint and throw out a guess — a few here or there, maybe, but not many. In fact, most will tell you their organizations *operate* on common sense. *Look how smoothly our office is running. The new IT system is much better than the old one (though it's already slightly outdated). We're thriving. We're* more *than thriving. If you have any doubts, check out our latest quarterly report, and you'll see how happy Wall Street is with our progress.*

But the truth, at least in my experience, is that in large organizations, the number of common-sense issues actually runs a lot higher; in a lot of cases, it's off the charts. The bigger the organization, the more common-sense issues there typically are. And if you take time to ask around and talk to employees, they will tell you that the IT department is a bunch of never-available nerds who find it beneath them to communicate with other departments and who have no time for anything, and you should read what customers say online about the company and its products and services, and who cares about the quarterly reports or Wall Street anyway because this company is kind of a nightmare.

They're not alone. Many of the examples you'll be reading about in this book, like the ones I gave earlier, may seem just too far-fetched to be real. But even though I have disguised individual and company names, I absolutely vouch for the fact that they do exist. So do these:

> When I ask the people in charge how many common-sense issues there are in their organizations, most say not many. The truth is that in large organizations, the number of common-sense issues is actually off the charts.

➤ At the height of the COVID pandemic, in order to reduce the possibility of transmission, a law was passed in Italy restricting the number of bathrooms that restaurants in Milan could have available to their customers. Restaurants complied, placing padlocks on all the cubicles except one. But what about diners who were waiting for their turn to use the bathroom? You guessed it: they had to line up to access the lone stall in the restaurants' narrow — and, nine times out of ten, packed — hallways.

I'm reminded of a flight I took from Zurich to Frankfurt around that same time period. Mindful of contagion, the Swiss regulatory authorities required all 180 passengers to fill out a form detailing our city of origin, where we were going, and even our seatmates' names, in case we, or they, later came down with a hacking cough, body aches, and fever. All 180 of us obliged, the problem being that the airline had only two pens, which for the next twenty minutes were passed up, down, and across aisles, from passenger to passenger, germy hand to germy hand.

The airline was meticulous about the disembarking process. One by one, by row letter — 1C, 2C, 3C — passengers rose, tightened their masks, collected their things, and exited the plane. Hand sanitizer was available for anyone who wanted it, and everyone kept a distance of six feet between them. At which point we were all herded like cows into a shuttle bus to take us to the terminal. Needless to say, the bus was elbow-to-elbow, facemask-to-facemask jammed.

➤ A company launched a new program designed to

"simplify" its various projects. The problem was that the company used literally thousands of acronyms — *Has the GLC come in yet, Drew, and does it confirm our SSNR? Is it RDF-compliant?* There were so many acronyms, employees couldn't keep them all straight. To help resolve the problem, the company self-published its own *Internal Acronym Dictionary* (or *IAD*). Aside from being incredibly boring to read, the *IAD* meant that whenever employees used an expression like "consumer packaged goods" (instead of CPG), they were scolded and told to look up the shorthand version. Looking up expressions and finding their matching acronyms soon became corporate law, or CL, as the company probably calls it.

➤ During a meeting, a vendor that sells equipment and parts to Home Depot was told there was too much swearing on the sales floor. When an employee pointed out that profanity was fairly common throughout the industry and that a lot of customers swore too, HR issued a company-wide memo: "swearing must now be confined to conversations between employees and customers."

➤ Where did it all go? In the first few weeks of the COVID-19 lockdown, toilet paper was as hard to come by as a Manhattan parking space. While people across the globe prepared for an indeterminate lockdown, photos and videos of naked toilet paper shelves in big-box stores appeared almost daily across social media, which incited even more hoarding and panic-buying. Even Amazon found itself behind on orders. Isn't it simply common sense for stores and their supply chains to factor in extreme events and keep enough toilet paper on hand, as the makers of other popular pandemic items — liquor, sex toys, greeting cards, weapons, coloring books, jigsaw puzzles, and Neflix subscriptions – discovered?

For those who found toilet paper only to lose their jobs, getting unemployment benefits proved to be even harder than landing work. All across the United States, employment checks arrived late, and sometimes not at all. When you called to find out where your check was, hoping an actual person could explain why your application was being held up, or why your entire account was locked, you were usually rewarded halfway through your multi-hour wait by the electronic system abruptly hanging up on you.

Whether we're masked or unmasked, attending meetings in person or via Zoom or Microsoft Teams, in the midst of a pandemic or in the aftermath of one, as you will see the absence of common sense shows up wherever humans beings come together. More than anything, I hope that the pages ahead reveal that the frustrations, constraints, headaches, tangles, and handcuffs you face every day aren't necessarily confined to your own workplace. Take it from me that this dumb stuff happens all around the world.

In the chapters that follow, in addition to presenting even more hard-to-believe but true cases of a lack of common sense in a variety of business and customer-centric settings, I also try to provide a road map to how you set up your own Ministry of Common Sense where you work.

To me, this makes all the sense in the world. In fact, it's just *common sense*.

1

WHY WON'T MY TV TURN ON?

BY NOW YOU'RE PROBABLY BEGINNING TO UNDERSTAND, as I have, that the disappearance of common sense in businesses of all sizes and shapes has become widespread, deepseated, and a little depressing. But where did common sense go? And how has the lack of it led to, among other things, the TSA prohibiting the use of knives on planes (though per TSA's website, feel free to bring aboard antlers, artificial skeleton bones, bocce balls, and bread machines); the Italian government passing a law banning round ice cubes since they can be used as weapons (the square ones can too, but never mind); or the sign I saw once in an Asian bathroom that read, DON'T STAND ON THE TOILET SEAT WHILE USING. These daily assaults against common sense don't just waste time, sap energy, and incite fury, they're also expensive. One consultancy found that old regulations and procedures put into place years ago and not updated since now cost companies

$15 billion annually in development and compliance—on top of the $94 billion it takes for companies to administer the compliance of these same rules internally.

This is why, in almost all the client organizations I work for, I've begun to establish a department I call the Ministry of Common Sense, devoted to overturning the frustrations, hurdles, and roadblocks within corporations that most leaders and managers don't even know are there. And by the way, the Ministry isn't some cloying, whimsical, feel-good jurisdiction either. It's not a Band-Aid. It's *real,* and it serves as the first line of defense against the thoughtless, at-times-incoherent systems, processes, rules, and regulations that squander resources, morale, and productivity.

Today I travel the world, transforming organizational cultures from the inside out. But it wasn't always that way. Until a few years ago, for the past two decades, I worked exclusively as a global branding expert and consultant. Looking back, the work I did for Microsoft, Pepsi, Burger King, Lego, Google, and other companies focused mainly on veneer issues. I loved my work, but upon reflection, it was also hit-and-run. Often I would come up with an idea, and knowing it was up to the organization to pass or reject it, I'd move on to the next thing. Now and then I suspected that the odds of my idea eventually bearing fruit were fifty-fifty, no matter how good I thought it was. But that was the company's problem, not mine.

A good illustration of this happened in 2005, when McDonald's hired me to transform its Happy Meal.

For the few of you who don't know, a McDonald's Happy Meal is the kids' version of what it sells to adult customers. Kids choose between a hamburger, cheeseburger, and Chicken McNuggets, all of which come with a small order of French fries, a soda, and a toy linked either to a TV show or movie. It's an efficient, inexpensive way to feed children, though not exactly what you'd call slimming or nutritious. At the time, every global trend was saying the same thing: "real" food was in, and fast and processed foods were on the way out. More and more articles linked fast food to childhood obesity, not just in the United States but across Europe, the Middle East, and Japan as well. Morgan Spurlock's film *Super Size Me* had just come out, chronicling the debilitating effects that eating only McDonald's food for a month had on the director's physical and mental health. Due to all of these concerns, I took the McDonald's job on one condition — that I could create a healthy alternative to the Happy Meal that also stimulated kids' imaginations. I ended up with a concept I called the Fantasy Meal, which I designed around one single purpose: to make toddlers eat broccoli.

The Fantasy Meal was actually *good* for kids. In one version, a small dragon held out a hamburger bun in its claws, with the hamburger itself nearby. I made stairs out of cucumber strips and carrot sticks. Another version was a replica of a space shuttle, with a tomato slice in the pilot's seat and carrot sticks framing the cockpit doors. I thought my Fantasy Meal concepts were pretty good. By creating environmentally friendly, nutritious meals for children, McDonald's would get a lot of credit for addressing a growing cultural and social issue. Kids would eat better. Parents would be happy. Everyone would win.

The response I received was extremely positive. *In-ter-est-ing!* I heard over and over again. I took this as a positive, not knowing that when a businessperson tells you your idea is *in-ter-est-ing,* you might as well jump off the roof. Yes, *in-ter-est-ing* occasionally means just that. But the rest of the time, *in-ter-est-ing* means that the people at the company a) hate your idea; b) hate your idea but can maybe figure out how to convince their colleagues that it's decent; or c) like your idea, sort of, but know there's no chance top management will ever go for it.

For the next few months, the Fantasy Meal idea shuffled around McDonald's global offices. People there gave feedback and proposed small changes — *but please know we still find the idea so in-ter-est-ing!* Almost a year later the Fantasy Meal concept came back to me.

When you were a kid, did you ever have the experience of losing your mother in a crowded supermarket? You burst into tears. Then you see her from behind and run forward, crying *"Mommmm!,"* only to have the woman turn around, and it's not your mom at all. It's just some other lady. Well, when my Fantasy Meal concept came back to me, it was some other lady. Gone were the dragon, the cucumber-strip stairs, the tomato-seat cushions, the carrot-stick columns. But there *was* a small apple!

Evidently, there were internal issues around how much the Fantasy Meal would cost to implement. Issues around building new factories and hiring labor to prepare all these fruits and vegetables, not to mention installing new equipment in all its restaurants. I can't remember what else, but the answer from McDonald's was *no.*

The company was, and still is, selling a few billion burgers a year. Why mess with a successful formula? Have an apple with your fries, kids, and don't forget to exercise more.

It was an *in-ter-est-ing* idea, though!

The more I asked around, the more it appeared that compromised, watered-down concepts — ones that often begin promisingly but then turn to mush — were an actual *thing*. A *phenomenon*. Not only that, the way people were doing business had changed, too, and not for the better. More and more companies were now investing in state-of-the-art technology systems, designed to automate everyday drudgeries and free employees to use their brains. Systems and processes were now dictating how employees spent their time and used their energy. A swarm of KPIs (Key Performance Indicators, which are numbers or values companies use to assess how performance measures up against overall objectives) was introduced to quantify everything a company did, which had the unfortunate effect of undermining and destabilizing cross-departmental problem-solving. Customer satisfaction gradually went down, and so did employee morale. This was happening all across the world too. It altered what, until then, had been the more or less linear arc of my own career.

> If a business is, at its core, a group of people networked together under a common purpose, everywhere I looked those networks seemed to be coming undone. And the first and most obvious casualty in all of this was common sense.

Maybe, I thought, the problem wasn't with the concepts. Maybe it was with the *organizations* and the *cultures*. If a business is, at its core, a group of people networked together under a common purpose, everywhere I looked those networks seemed to be coming undone. And the first and most obvious casualty in all of this was common sense.

As I went from company to company, I gradually assembled my own five-part program for restoring some semblance of common sense to corporate organizations. It takes time. It's the opposite of an overnight fix. Because when people start working inside organizations, something *happens* to them. They forget they're human. They start adhering to rules, processes, procedures, and official and unofficial codes of behavior that make no sense to anyone outside the organization. Somewhere along the line they forget how they would feel if a bank told them their checking account was frozen or if their "customer care" call involved four different departments and tore a ninety-minute hole in their lives while being told repeatedly that "this call is being recorded for training purposes." Usually an outsider is needed to come in and repair things to which businesses have become blind.

Alan Mulally, the former CEO of Ford, once told me that during his first two weeks on the job, he knew his company had gone off the rails when he found that the majority of the cars in the employee parking lot were . . . well, not Ford cars!

The good news is that by restoring common sense to organizations, employees are beginning to see the world through more human eyes and, along the way, to rebuild their companies' brand.

Imagine that, as a consumer, you order a pair of flats online. They show up in the wrong size. When you can't find the return postage label (because there isn't one), you jam them inside an old wine carton and pay $17 at your local post office to send them back. Two weeks go by without any acknowledgment from the company. When you call to inquire about a refund or exchange – and the customer service phone number isn't listed on the website because the last thing the company *wants* is for you to call them – you're placed on hold three times as you get transferred from one department to the next. You put your phone on mute, and start yelling, vowing never to buy shoes from that company again. In fact, you vow never to *wear* shoes again if it's going to be this much of a hassle.

As an employee, is this the kind of service you would want or expect if something similar happened to you? Would this experience lead you to recommend the shoe company to friends and family members? I doubt it. (Consider that if each employee knows at least twenty people and a company has tens of thousands of employees, the recommendations alone are enough to turn many organizations around.) Alan Mulally, the former CEO of Ford, once told me that during his first two weeks on the job, he knew his company had gone off the rails when he found that the majority of the cars in the employee parking lot were . . . well, not Ford cars!

In the end, improved efficiency, productivity, morale, and happiness all come back to how much common sense there is inside an organization. The lack of common sense in turn has a significant effect on items you would never expect, such as your TV remote control.

I was in Miami a couple of years ago for a conference, staying at a hotel. Wanting to check the day's headlines, I reached for the TV remote. It was remarkably complex. It looked like it could launch a rocket ship, actually. Infinite tiny numbers. A multitude of buttons. Three separate numerical keypads. Where was the ON button? Was it the red one labeled "On"?

Wait — why were there *two* red ON buttons? If I pressed both, would my TV be *incredibly* on, allowing me to access supernatural programming that viewers with just one ON button couldn't? What did "Source" mean? What did "a-b-c-d" mean? What did all the arrows signify? After stabbing indiscriminately at the thing for a few minutes, the TV finally came to life. I watched the news for a few minutes, then shut the TV off, or tried to. There were two OFF buttons. When I pressed the first one, the lights in the room dimmed in a moody, sexy way. When I pressed the second OFF button, the air conditioner shut off. The TV stayed on. I ended up climbing up onto a nearby desk and, with my butt in the air, yanking the plugs from the wall socket, disconnecting the TV, the minibar, and the standing lamp.

A few months later, during a flight to New York, the passenger seated next to me introduced himself. It turned out, purely by coincidence, that he was an engineer at the very same company responsible for that TV remote. "You've probably never heard of the company," he said. "Want to bet?" I said.

Powering up my laptop, I showed him the PowerPoint slide I'd made of the remote control. "What the hell went wrong with you guys?" I said. He stiffened in his seat. He explained that the company had internal problems, with various divisions vying for real estate on the remote control. No one could agree which department "owned" what. Ultimately the TV remote was divided up into zones resembling each of the internal departments in his company. One was for the TV. A second was for cable. A third was for TiVo. A fourth was for satellite. A fifth belonged to the folks responsible for broadcasting big band era or hip-hop music 24/7, or for displaying a crackling yule log in winter. The engineer seemed proud of what his company had done and how equitably things had been resolved. There were no more internal squabbles. Every division now had fair representation on the remote. "Except for the fact I have no idea how to turn the TV on!" I said. He looked at me, still not understanding.

How does an overcomplicated remote control circle back to an absence of common sense in an organization? Very simply. As the engineer sitting next to me pointed out, the average TV remote control — with its logographic script of arrows, keys, buttons, numbers, and letters — reflects any number of internal miscommunications and power struggles inside a local telecom. Just as a footbridge with a small crack along one side can indicate more serious foundational problems, an unintuitive remote control points to a few core problems within the company that issued it. With half a dozen silos inside the cable company vying for representation, no one was looking at the remote control holistically — that is, from the consumer's point of view.

Those internal corporate divisions probably don't even speak to one another. That's why we as consumers reach for

> The TV remote control in my hotel room had infinite tiny numbers, a multitude of buttons, and three separate numerical keypads. Why were there two ON buttons? What did "a-b-c-d" mean? Why couldn't I, a forty-nine-year-old man, figure out how to turn on the TV?

this slender, schizophrenic plastic monster with such confusion, irritation, and anger. Because the root cause of a lack of common sense generally comes down to a series of disconnects among organizations, employees, and consumers. The worst part? Time after time we end up blaming *ourselves* as though it's our fault that we can't figure out the remote.

This is just one example of how the objects surrounding us inevitably refer back to bigger, commonsensical issues inside organizations. You'll be reading about more of them in this book. It might be Waze announcing that the highways near me are jammed and redirecting me to a small side road, which means that along with hundreds of other Waze users, I'm now trapped in an eight-mile-long traffic jam on a small side road. It could be airlines asking you to raise your window shades (a safety regulation rule?) or lower them (something to do with the environment?). Or those same airlines limiting the liquids passengers can bring aboard inside a carry-on bottle to just one ounce, overlooking the fact that by combining the contents of all those one-ounce bottles into one big bottle, a person could create enough liquid to . . . you know. Or the fact that an online form for the U.S. Department of Homeland Security asks applicants, "Are you a terrorist?" and includes a box they can check if the answer is "I sure am!" Or the fact that some credit card machines make you swipe, others make you insert, some make you sign, others don't. Or to avoid waiting in a long line, you order tickets online to a concert or event, only to find out that the only way to pick up those tickets is . . . by standing in a long line at the box office. Or the fact that one company I know requires employees to submit their sick-day requests twenty-four hours before they call in sick (physiologically, I'm not sure how this works). I could go on, and I will too. Almost every stupidity and inconvenience we face as consumers can be traced back directly to a faulty or broken corporate ecosystem — one that has abandoned, for whatever reason, a few fundamental principles of common sense.

2

WHERE HAS EMPATHY GONE?

To facilitate the scheduling of meetings, a major corporation installed an online calendar system. That way, employees could easily find their colleagues' open time slots. People eagerly began booking meetings with one another, which had the effect of clogging up everyone else's calendars. So, to prevent complete strangers from booking their time, employees also began plugging in fake meetings, resulting in no more open time slots. As a workaround, thousands of employees got together to create a paper version of their secret calendars, where they keep track of their *real* appointments.

So, where's the common sense in installing an expensive online calendar system when it leads to less productivity and employees now having to literally call one another to find out if they have any time available?

HAVE YOU AND A FRIEND EVER WALKED into a deserted restaurant in the middle of the afternoon and requested a table? I want you to picture a vast, lovely room, made lovelier because it's so empty, all the tables set with placemats, silverware, napkins, and water glasses. The maître d' greets you, and when you tell him there'll be two for lunch, he says, "Of course. If you'll give me o-n-n-n-ne second while I check . . ."

He taps a few numbers into his computer. *Plink-plink-plink.* Every table in the restaurant is empty, there's literally no one else around, so what could he possibly be doing? Why doesn't he just say, "Take your pick!" or "Guys, please, go nuts!" Instead he stares into the screen with narrowing eyes before tapping in a few more keys. Is he finishing his dissertation? Is he writing a screenplay? Turning now, he surveys the room. It's as if he's seeing something your eyes don't – an overflowing crowd of smartly dressed diners with their heads thrown back merrily. He gazes at you in a knowing way. "Follow me." Picking up two menus, he leads you across the room, depositing you and your friend at a table two feet away from the bathroom. Well, at least it's convenient. *"Enjoy,"* he says.

"Wow, thanks so much for your help," you say.

It's harder to acknowledge when something is missing than to see it when it's right in front of you – a statement that's certainly true as far as common sense is concerned. Before going any further, let's define what common sense is and isn't. It's tricky, because common sense is so unconscious, and so foundational to the choices we make every day, that we seldom stop and wonder how we learned to look both ways before crossing the street or turn down the thermostat at night or any of a hundred other things that routinely fall under the category of common sense.

Common sense refers to the judgment and instinct that has been shaped and refined by experience, observation, intelligence, and intuition. It has evolved from centuries of human experience — of you, me, and our forebears observing behavior patterns, avoiding threats to our health, warding off fears, and maintaining our safety, sanity, and well-being. Common sense is the *sum total* of our ability to separate right from wrong, efficient from inefficient, useful from pointless, valuable from worthless, orderly from sloppy, clean from dirty, dry from soaked, secure from hazardous, mature from childish, beneficial from harmful, and prudent from ill-advised. Common sense is practical. It's reasonable. It's iterative. It's dynamic. It's obvious or, rather, it's *supposed* to be obvious. When it's working, common sense often leads to a sense of happiness, productivity, and an improved quality of life. When it's *not* working, you want to tear your hair out.

In general, our parents and teachers are responsible for teaching us the fundamentals of common sense. It's a gradual, ongoing education that starts when we're young. *Eat your vegetables. Don't hit your sister. Wear socks. Change your underwear. Brush your teeth. Use an umbrella if it's raining.* Eventually we get exposed to even more common-sense principles from our friends and siblings, from TV shows, movies, and books, and from our own school-of-life experiences. Very quickly common sense becomes unconscious. So does the *or else* clause implicit in common sense.

For example, it's common sense to bathe and put on de-odorant (or else no one will want to be around us); to eat three meals a day (or else we'll be hungry) and save dessert for last (because . . . that's just the way it works); to not pet strange dogs (or else they'll bite us); to save our money (or else we'll run out of it); to exercise (or else we'll get fat); to drink wa-ter instead of sugary sodas (see above, plus cavities); to get eight hours of sleep at night (or else we'll be unproductive the next day); to wear warm clothes in the winter (or else we'll get cold); to turn off the burners before leaving the house (or else we'll have a gas explosion and/or our house will burn down); and so on. Trial and error plays a big role in the accumula-tion of common sense — *change the oil in your car; let the dog out; buy flowers on your wedding anniversary* — and so does technological hearsay: *Meet in a public setting on your first Tinder date* (or else your date might kill you). *Don't text and drive at the same time* (or else you'll crash into a tree). *Don't use 1234, the most frequently used password today, as your cell phone passcode* (or else a stranger might steal all your in-formation). *Don't post photos of your children on social me-dia* (or else I'm not sure what will happen, but nothing good).

Considering how much we're exposed to common sense throughout our lives, why is it so scarce in most organizations?

The author, Harriet Beecher Stowe, defined common sense as "Seeing things as they are; and doing things as they ought to be done." Wouldn't it follow that companies would *want* to treat consumers and employees as they themselves would expect to be treated? That they should behave in ways and create products and services that are reasonable, depend-able, down-to-earth, and practical, ensuring that common sense took center stage? You'd *think*, wouldn't you?

A well-known global investment firm (you'd know the name) has on staff up to a dozen "levels" of employees. Level 1 refers to tellers and customer service representatives, and up it goes from there, all the way to the top level, which is the CEO. Any manual payments made to clients requires a Level 4 employee (e.g., a senior person) to sign off on it. This rule means that the request has to first pass through Levels 1 to 3 (another rule says that a sign-off can't "jump" four levels but needs to be approved at each rung up the ladder).

Each level takes time, and therefore, nine times out of ten the payment is delayed. These delays in turn cause penalties for the customer. And penalties can only be signed off by — Yes! — a Level 4 employee. All this is done to reduce costs and minimize penalties. Causing even more delays and more penalties.

To my mind, a few factors lie behind the dissolution of common sense in the business world. I'll go into greater detail about each one of them later, but here they are in summary.

(BAD) CUSTOMER EXPERIENCE

I define customer experience as being every single touchpoint that enables a product or service to be delivered to you and me, whether it's online, in a store, or over the phone. Every employee contributes to great customer experience. The most successful organizations and brands in the world think and act in the interests of their customers by always putting themselves in *their* shoes.

You'd be surprised how rarely this happens. (Take my TV remote control or my headphones – please.) Most companies are accountable to Wall Street and their shareholders, period. They overlook the people who actually buy and use their products and services, forgetting that customer-centric organizations not only create value but drive sustainable growth. In this clash of priorities, common sense dies.

POLITICS

We can all probably agree that whenever ego, hierarchy, power, money, and people are involved, organizational politics will follow. I can always tell when politics are a problem in a company when: a) the business has multiple "levels"; b) geographical distances exist between company offices and employees; c) bosses habitually change their minds and opinions; d) the culture is dominated by silos; e) frequent internal communication is lacking; and f) few employees know what anyone else in the organization is doing and are instead focused on defending and preserving their own turf. Oftentimes in this scramble, common sense is among the first casualties.

TECHNOLOGY

There's no point in complaining about technology, but that doesn't mean I can't give it my best shot. Tech, of course, has invaded every aspect of our lives, and where it hasn't yet, it surely will in the next few years and decades. The value and convenience that technology creates are obvious and enthusiastically received most of the time. Or maybe we're all so beaten down by now we know it doesn't even matter what we think, that tech will keep advancing anyway, with or without us.

I'm hardly anti-tech. But more than any other factor, tech is the enemy of common sense. It destroys empathy, compromises our agency, turns grownups into children, impedes innovation, and, worst of all, makes us doubt our own store of common sense (the *human* kind). In 2016, the Bureau of Labor Statistics reported that even though Americans were working harder than ever, overall productivity had plummeted again, a losing streak that began in 2006. I can't prove it, but certainly technology has to bear *some* of the blame.

MEETINGS AND POWERPOINTS

If companies had their way, meetings would be scheduled from morning until night. Breakfast meetings, snack meetings, lunch meetings, midafternoon meetings, twilight meetings, dinner meetings, bedtime meetings. Most meetings start late, end late, and amount to little accomplishment. When the people there aren't doing everything in their power to impress their bosses and show their colleagues how smart, committed, and driven they are, they're preparing for the next meeting, and the one after that, and the PowerPoint presentation that they have to do . . .

Send me a deck. Is there anything more chilling than those four words? By now you probably know, as I do, that if someone asks you to send them a deck, they're already pretty *meh* on the idea, and when you *do* send one, chances are no one will read it. PowerPoints are mostly exercises in time wasted, productivity lost, and everyone simply going through the corporate motions.

RULES, REGULATIONS, AND POLICIES

It begins when we're young: *No swimming. Walking on the lawn is forbidden. No games allowed. Mind the gap. All passengers must show a valid ID.* Later, when we enter the workforce, rules, regulations, and policies multiply: *After 8 p.m., use the service elevator. All employees must be certified TG7-compliant. Please submit Form 76Z. Your request has been denied.* Online, it's just as bad: *After three failed attempts, your account will be frozen. Access to this page is denied. Your password must be at least six characters long and contain one capital letter, two numbers, 1½ cups chopped onion, two tablespoons all-purpose flour, and six ounces of skinless, boneless chicken.*

Most companies overflow with rules and policies, some official, others less so. Most are written as standalone documents. No one has ever reviewed them as a whole (because there are too damn many of them), just as not one of us bothers to read the privacy or compliance form that shows up after a software update or download. We simply check AGREE, and hope we haven't just signed our lives away. Worse, these rules have become part of company folklore. With no one able to get a handle on all of them, which would be impossible anyway, employees get scared. They begin imagining that using a pencil sharpener or applying lip gloss is "against company policy" or hasn't been approved yet by the top layer of an organization, because doesn't senior management always have to approve new policies?

COMPLIANCE AND LEGAL

It's only *your* company that's so gun-shy and rule-bound, right? No, actually it's *every* company. Which of us who works in an organization *doesn't* inhabit a system of rules, manuals, and restrictions established by compliance and legal departments that dictate everything from our wardrobe to how best to make small talk with customers?

But if employees are continually told to adhere to company statutes and edicts and to ignore what their "gut instinct" is telling them, they lose all agency—and surrender their own humanity. As a result, ordinances win and common sense loses.

One of the largest cities in America asked itself, "What if every citizen in this metropolis had access to Wi-Fi?" It was a good, and overdue, idea, certainly one that would attract entrepreneurs and new businesses to the city's many skyscrapers and office buildings. Soon, hundreds of routers were installed across the city, on trees, poles, and elsewhere, most, if not all, forty-five feet above the sidewalk. That's about three stories high. Unfortunately, the city seemed not to know, or had forgotten, that routers broadcast down, not up. As a result, everyone in a house or an office below the three-story level had a crystal-clear Wi-Fi signal. For anyone who worked above the third floor in any building, there were barely any bars at all.

Before we go any further with common sense, I want to clarify something important. So far, I've defined it as sensible, reasonable, practical, and down-to-earth. Common sense means that you use good judgment when making decisions. You conduct your life at home and at work in a manner that's both sane and prudent. You know what to do and how to respond intuitively and automatically, not from study or some arcane body of knowledge but from basic human experience. Finally, you're able to assess a situation or a set of facts and then make a sound and sensible judgment. But you know all that . . . right!

Common sense is all these things, to be sure. But the reason why we see less and less of it in the world now isn't as straightforward as you think. In my experience, the lack of common sense in companies (and in life) has a clear, if indirect, connection to the increasing disappearance of *empathy*.

If this sounds crazy, think back to the common-sense principles I mentioned earlier, the ones handed down to us by our parents and teachers. *Use an umbrella when it rains. Brush your teeth. Say "please" and "thank you." Offer your seat to a pregnant woman, or an older person, on the bus or subway.* Isn't the essence of common

> In my experience, the lack of common sense in companies (and in life) has a clear, if indirect, connection to the increasing disappearance of *empathy*.

sense putting yourself in another person's shoes and feeling what *they* feel?

After all, you know what it's like to be without an umbrella. You know how it feels when a car comes close to brushing you in a crosswalk, or when you forget to lock your back door or shut off the stove, or what can happen if you don't say "please" or "thank you." Don't you want to keep other people, especially kids, from making these same mistakes? As rational as it sounds on the surface, at its heart, common sense involves caring, connecting, and emotional identification. Common sense is all about empathy.

Now, maybe needless to say, I don't talk much about empathy when I'm inside organizations. Corporate types usually associate the term with sentimentality or crying or cupcakes. It seems to have no apparent fit in formal circles. That's why, whenever I address common-sense issues in businesses, I use a concept that I borrowed from a Hollywood director.

Along with being remembered for his films, Alfred Hitchcock was known for his atypical approach to scriptwriting. For example, for every movie he wrote and directed, he compiled two separate screenplays: a blue script and a green script. The blue script resembled a traditional three-act screenplay, with dialogue, cues, camera angles, camera shots, and stage directions. Is this the point when James Stewart looks out the window to see his neighbor cleaning a knife? *Blue script*. Where should Tippi Hedren stand as those birds attack her? *Blue script*. The green script, on the other hand, focused on what Hitchcock wanted audiences to feel, on a minute-by-minute and even second-by-second basis. Apprehension. Anxiety. Fear. Shock. Relief.

In a company, if a blue script describes the causes (e.g., operational inefficiencies), the green script shows the overall effects (e.g., a lack of common sense). If a blue script highlights those departments that aren't working together or those systems or processes that get in the way of productivity, a green script reveals where common sense (and a lot of the time, empathy) is missing. It could be the customer service center that shuffles callers to eleven different departments or the weekly, hourlong meeting that exists purely for its own sake.

Again, if the blue script — fact-based, unambiguous, and measurable — focuses on day-to-day problems, stoppages, or miscommunications, the green script focuses on the effects of those problems, most often a lack of common sense and empathy: empathy among various departments or silos; empathy between senior and middle management; empathy between employees and consumers.

What *is* empathy? It's our ability to feel what other people feel and experience what they experience. People use the words "sympathy" and "empathy" interchangeably, but in workshops I usually illustrate their differences this way:

Imagine you and I are on an ocean voyage together. It's stormy outside, and the ocean is choppy. I catch sight of you standing on one of the outside decks. You're bent over, your face is white, and you're gripping the railing with both hands. A moment later I watch

> The difference between "sympathy" and "empathy" is the difference between me seeing you throw up and handing you a napkin and me seeing you throw up and feeling so bad about how you're feeling that I throw up myself.

you throw up over the side. If I joined you on the deck, said, "Wow, poor you," and handed you a napkin, I would be show-ing sympathy; if I stood beside you on the deck and threw up myself, that would be empathy.

Sympathy, then, means that we can identify with what an-other person is going through. We feel sympathetic toward someone whose mom has just died, a friend who's just been laid off, or a family we read about who lost their home in a hurricane. Sympathy doesn't go much deeper than that. Of-ten it shows up as the veneer of polite interest we show others — friends, neighbors, shopkeepers — on a day-to-day basis. In America and the United Kingdom, for example, sympathy is practically a cultural dictate.

Years ago, during my first or second visit to the United States when I was still trying to make sense of the country's unofficial rules of engagement and making mistakes left and right, I remember checking into a hotel when a bellman in-quired politely, "How are you, sir?" I'll never forget the can-did, heartfelt, tortured, overly elaborate response I gave about, well, how I truly was. (Overly elaborate because ap-parently the only right answer was to simply say "Fine.") He looked a little scared — he probably thought I needed a full medical workup — and grew silent.

A year ago when I was in London, something similar hap-pened but in reverse. Someone asked, "How are you doing?" and as an experiment I answered that things actually *weren't* going all that well and that my dad had just died. (Which was true.) "Good to hear it," he said without breaking stride. "I see you brought the good weather with you." This confirmed my belief that sympathy usually serves as the thinnest decorative covering over our daily encounters and that there's not much else behind it.

(I've often noticed when I'm flying that whenever I ask for a glass of sparkling water with ice and lemon, the airline attendants will invariably bobble my order, probably because they've heard one like it so many times. They either forget the ice or the lemon, or they give me a glass of regular water instead. To prevent this from happening, I now tell them I'd like a glass of ice, with lemon and sparkling water. It's such a weird order that they actually bring it to me.)

Empathy is deeper, more intimate and less boundaried than sympathy, less a default reflex than an act of identification. When we empathize with a friend who has just gone through a terrible work experience or a breakup, we actually imagine *being* our friend. Empathy allows us to imagine how we would feel if it happened to *us*.

As infants, we're programmed to imitate one another. It's how we learn things. Stick your tongue out at a newborn baby, and the baby will immediately stick out his or her tongue at you. When our mothers smile at us as infants, we smile back. If one of our little friends scrapes his arm or twists her ankle, we "feel" what they're feeling. Other people yawn, and we yawn back, almost a call-and-response. Just by reading the word "yawn," you and I are more likely to yawn. What goes through your mind when you read the words, "Long nails scratching against a blackboard"? We instinctively cringe. The nails/blackboard sound produces a sensation known as "grima," used to describe sounds that repel us or are unpleasant in some way. This, and other irritating sounds (a knife clinking or dragging against a plate) are in the middle of the human audio range, a frequency, one study speculates, that mimics the shrill warning cries of our chimpanzee ancestors. It goes back *that* far. (I was once discussing a new shampoo in a GlaxoSmithKline focus group when everyone in the room began scratching their heads simultaneously.) In short, our survival as humans depends on empathy — on understanding what other people are feeling and doing.

I was reminded of this a few years ago when I was working with Nestlé, helping them launch a line of organic baby food in France. NaturNes was the purest, healthiest bio baby food on the market — no salt, no sugar, no chemicals, no stabilizers — but for some reason, it wasn't selling. Nestlé had spent a lot of money on the product, and no one could understand why French babies were spitting it out. When I traveled around France interviewing consumers, I soon found out why. New mothers usually sample what they're feeding their babies, and then smile, showing them how good it tastes. Primed by their mothers' expressions, babies eat up. This time around, I focused my attention on the moms. As they sampled NaturNes, they looked dismayed. Clearly, they hated the stuff. It was too bland. It didn't have enough seasoning. The babies responded by spitting the food out. Nestlé had to go back and rethink their approach.

With a few exceptions, the capacity for empathy is innate. Babies cry when they hear other babies cry. A child will offer his pacifier to another child who doesn't have one. But empathy is also learned. If your parents responded to you empathically when you were little, your own capacity for empathy grew. If they ignored you or brushed you off, your empathy levels probably stagnated. Still, no matter how old we are, the more we interact with other people, the more empathic we become. And that's the problem.

Empathy, in fact, is on the decline, at least among college students. According to the *New York Times*, a University of Michigan research team looked at four pillars of what they called "interpersonal sensitivity" among 14,000 college students from 1980 to 2010. They measured the range from the compassion or anguish students feel over other people's misfortunes to their capacity to imagine the perspective of other people, including fictional characters from books and movies. "Students scored significantly lower in empathic concern (a 48 percent decrease) and perspective taking (34 percent)" the *Times* reported, adding that the University of Michigan team found that "a millennial mixture of video games, social media, reality TV and hyper-competition have left young people self-involved, shallow and unfettered in their individualism and ambition."

The University of Michigan did their empathy study in 2010. In the decade since, I suspect that empathy has slipped even further away. With our phones creating a barrier between us and the world, we don't notice things anymore. Our phones have become shields, lightsabers, transitional objects, and phantom limbs. They defend against our fear, anxiety, loneliness, self-consciousness, sadness, and insignificance. If we're in a bar and our date hasn't shown up yet, we pick up our phones and do something, *anything*, just so we don't look as pathetic as we feel.

According to a 2019 report conducted by Common Sense Media, 26 percent of parents now use a smartphone or tablet within five minutes of going to sleep. Around the same percentage woke up at least once during the night to check their phones, and 23 percent reached for a phone or tablet within five minutes of awakening. Use among adolescents is even higher. Forty percent of adolescents check their phone or tablet before going to bed, 36 percent wake up in the middle of the night to check texts and calls, and 32 percent grab their phones within five minutes of waking up.

In another study from a few years ago, just the *presence* of a phone on a table while two people had a ten-minute conversation was shown to decrease empathy levels. The researchers put it this way: "Conversations in the absence of mobile communication technologies were rated as significantly superior compared with those in the presence of a mobile device, above and beyond the effects of age, gender, ethnicity, and mood." They added, "People who had conversations in the absence of mobile devices reported higher levels of empathetic concern."

Some enterprising AI companies are now even trying to import empathy digitally. Cogito, a Boston-based company, places hearts in the corner of a screen when a customer service representative isn't showing enough "heart." These and other visual notifications—a speedometer if a call is taking too long, a cup of coffee if the customer service rep sounds sluggish—are showing up in more and more call centers, including MetLife's—and if workers somehow shrink or ignore these prompts, Cogito notifies their supervisor.

Scan the headlines of websites and newspapers in almost any country, and you'll read how polarized populations have become. Why now? We have less empathy—and zero sympathy—for people who disagree with us about politics, crime, race, abortion, or sexual preferences. The rise of social media also means it's more and more unacceptable to display human vulnerability. Perfection, or the perception of perfection, destroys empathy. Online, everyone is ideal, happy, and wealthy. Their friends are fun and glamorous, and they really love being around you! When your friends on social media aren't having cocktail parties, they're traveling. Italy, Turks and Caicos, the Basque region. Or they're taking a selfie in a Dutch tulip field, not noticing or really caring that they're crushing the tulips under their feet. Almost never do we glimpse any weaknesses, flaws, or humanity in the lives of our online friends, or reveal any of our own.

That's why it always comes as a shock when we actually meet up with the friends we've been tracking on social media. Over lunch, they'll tell you they just survived a close scare with cancer; they're on their fifth antidepressant in a year; their daughter is in rehab; and their son-in-law can't find a job. The only possible response is "I would never have guessed." A good friend of mine told me she'd actually lost friends thanks to social media — that she'd gotten so used to reading about their lives in their feeds, she'd completely forgotten about emailing or calling them.

If empathy is linked so strongly to common sense, how does its disappearance affect companies? The answer is that businesses today have squeezed out almost everything that could be called "human." If something can't be measured or quantified, it doesn't exist. If it does, data determines if it's right or wrong. If an email bounces back or our laptops can't connect with a server, *we're* the ones at fault. If Google Maps tells us the street address we typed in doesn't exist, we assume we were off by a digit, that it's somehow *our* fault.

What's right, what's wrong? Check the manual or the

instruction booklet. Ask HR. Consult legal and compliance. In the early 2000s, I led focus groups for Lego. I would sit on the floor with a group of little kids and build Lego castles with them. Once their castles were finished, kids stuck a flag on the top. *All done.* But when I do this same experiment today and position the flag an inch to the left or right of center, the kids tell me I'm *wrong. The flag goes* here! *The instruction manual* says *so! It doesn't work when you place the flag in the wrong spot!*

With empathy eroding, businesses pay a price. Empathy, after all, is what distinguishes a consumer who is loyal for life from another who swears she'll never go near your company again. I once interviewed an executive who told me about a shopping experience he'd witnessed while he was waiting in line in a large European electronics chain. In an effort to show more awareness around environmental sustainability, the store had initiated a new rule: if customers wanted a plastic bag at checkout, they would have to pay for it. As the executive was waiting in line, he noticed the woman in front of him. She was buying thousands of dollars of stuff — a laptop, a printer, headphones, and so on.

As her credit card went through, the woman realized she needed a plastic bag for her incidentals. "That'll be one dollar," the male clerk said. But the woman had no money or change on her. "I'll just put it on my credit card," she said, only to be told by the clerk that there was a $5 minimum for all credit card transactions with no exceptions. She had just bought thousands of dollars of electronic equipment! She was so angry she returned everything in her cart and told the clerk she would never shop there again. Who can blame her?

Last year I hosted a company party at a five star hotel in

Mallorca, Spain. When our party was assembled, I found out that the bar closed at midnight — which is weird, considering most Spaniards don't even start dining until 9 or 10 p.m. Blaming some complex international regulations, the hotel told me there would be no liquor service after 12 a.m. and no room service after 10:30 p.m. This was news to me — bad news. The next day our entire party checked out, days earlier than planned; we had found rooms a block away, where the bar didn't close until 2 a.m. and common sense hadn't gone completely haywire. In the end, the hotel gave up tens of thousands of dollars in revenue all because of some stupid, arbitrary, global — but locally insensitive — rule.

On the other hand, there are also great customer experiences, like the one I had a few years ago when I ordered a cup of sake at a Tokyo bar. In Japan, sake is typically served in a miniature glass placed inside a wooden box. An older woman appeared out of nowhere and began pouring the sake. And pouring. She kept pouring sake until it spilled over the sides of the glass and into the box. When I asked her why she'd just done that, she told me that the Japanese have a tradition of giving more than what is expected — to underpromise and overdeliver and to create a sense of surprise. It's one of the secrets behind every great or memorable consumer experience, and why is it even a secret?

Businesses that ignore empathy not only kill common sense, they also place future innovation at risk.

3

OUTSIDE IN, *NOT* INSIDE OUT

LAST YEAR, I HAD TO FLY FROM Dubai to Romania for business. An hour and a half before our flight left, a colleague and I checked in at Emirates airlines at Dubai International Airport. Or rather, we tried to. "You must be some kind of Olympic athlete," the masked ticket agent said, explaining that our flight was scheduled to leave from another terminal. In most airports, you would just board a bus or a plane train and ten minutes later you would be at your gate. But the second Emirates terminal was so far away from this one, the agent said, that even if I managed to find a taxi, I wouldn't reach my gate until the plane was on the runway.

My colleague and I were resigned to missing our flight when the agent then proposed another idea: if I ran — seriously, *ran* — along a network of back landings, passing in and out of security checks, I could get to my gate in forty-five minutes. He must have seen our expressions. "It's my lunch break," he said. "I'll run with you. I could use the exercise."

Armed with our luggage trolley, the three of us jogged up and down stairwells and along deserted corridors, dodging in and out of a half-dozen security checks. Whenever there was a holdup or a long line ahead of us, the agent flashed his badge (and stretched the truth now and then), and we were waved through. Forty-five minutes later, out of breath, we reached the Emirates gate.

Why would any employee do that? Empathy. He was treating me as he would wish to be treated if he were in our situation. From a common-sense standpoint, he was ensuring my loyalty to the airline for the rest of my life. It's no more nor less than the Golden Rule, of which one variation or another dates back to 500 BC: *Treat others as you would like to be treated.* Or, in its more negative form, *Do not treat others in ways you would not like to be treated yourself.*

Whenever I run workshops, I ask employees to describe their best, most memorable customer service experience. Regardless of whether I'm in Switzerland, Russia, Thailand, or North Carolina, the same three qualities show up again and again. First, the experience happened when the consumer was in a time of real need. She was sick, or her child was sick, or she'd lost her luggage, or her glasses had broken and she didn't have a backup pair, or she'd left her phone behind in a hotel room or on a plane. Second, the employee she dealt with fully empathized with what she was going through. Third, he or she went beyond their prescribed roles to solve the problem.

Most of the time this doesn't happen. Why? Simple. Companies never sit down and talk to their customers. People who work in organizations forget that *they're* consumers too. Time and again this disconnect immediately short-circuits common sense.

The issue comes up in my line of work again and again. Just last year, for example, shortly after I began working with Cath Kidston, a popular London-based clothing and lifestyle brand, the management team and I met for an early morning workshop. The company had provided pens and notepads, wrapped tightly in plastic. Nearby was a selection of boxes filled with Cath Kidston products, also bound in plastic. To save time, I asked the early arrivals to unwrap all the pens, pads, and boxes. It took five of them more than half an hour to finish the job.

"How consumer-focused are you?" I asked Cath Kidston employees when the workshop began. They assured me that the consumer was the company's number one priority. "Do Cath Kidston consumers care about the environment?" *Yes, absolutely,* came the replies. "Well," I said, "when you're not at work, you are also *consumers* who probably order a lot of things online. What would you say is your biggest frustration when a package shows up in the mail?"

The response was almost unanimous: *Too much plastic. Too much unwrapping.* One woman told me she'd once spent almost an hour trying to extract three shirts from their cardboard container. "Has anyone else here had that same experience?" I asked. Everyone raised their hands. I asked them to take note of their colleagues, who'd been tasked to unwrap the very same boxes that show up at Cath Kidston retail stores, which employees then spent hours unwrapping.

Not just pens and pads but bags, cups, plates, shirts, dresses, and dozens of other products. Sustainability issues aside, the company was squandering its own employees' time and productivity.

In short, a little common sense would have gone a long way.

This is a core reason why I bring employees together with customers in consumers' homes whenever I start working with a company. For the first time, employees are given an opportunity to see the world from the outside in, as their *customers* see it, instead of seeing the world from the inside out. If your company sells products or services, doesn't it make sense to figure out who your customers are and what they want?

A few years ago, I did an experiment with the senior members of a telecommunications company in Medellín, Colombia. None of them had ever experienced what it might be like to be a customer in one of their stores. The rule was that no customer should ever be obliged to wait in line more than fifty-nine minutes. (If you're wondering why the company didn't just round it off to sixty minutes, the government exacts a penalty on companies if customers wait an hour or longer.) Now, fifty-nine minutes sounds wearying enough, but in this case, it was also a mind game, a trick to drive telecom customers half mad.

Imagine that you're one of them. At the forty-eight-minute point of your fifty-nine-minute wait, an agent summons you to the counter. You're handed a ticket and told to stand in another line. The fifty-nine-minute clock then starts over. If, when you reach the counter, the customer service rep can't resolve your issue, you're transferred to a third line, and another fifty-nine-minute wait. This experience can last up to three hours. When I realized senior management staff members had no idea what their own customers went through, I invited half a dozen of them to meet me at a precise replica of the store inside a large local convention center.

With the goal of recreating the average customer experience as exactly as possible, I made sure that the temperature in the store was a balmy ninety-five degrees, as it is every day. Outside, on the sidewalk, I installed a team of men with machine guns (which wasn't an unusual sight in that particular neighborhood), while inside, forty or so customers sat in a row of old chairs, gazing with half-dead eyes at a TV that was broadcasting company infomercials. Every thirty seconds, a clock beeped to alert customers at the front of the line that it was their turn to approach the counter.

Two hours into this hell, one manager — red-faced, sweating profusely, and sick and tired of waiting for the workshop to begin — announced he was going back to the office. I told him this *was* the workshop, and he *couldn't* go back to the office. He retook his seat, unhappily, but for the first time something dawned on him. For the next two hours, the management team and I created a graph listing every excuse that telecom employees gave customers once they reached the counter. *Sorry, I can't help you. I'm afraid that's not my responsibility. Come back next Tuesday and bring this ticket. Here's our toll-free number. Sorry, but we don't accept that as a valid form of ID.*

The manager who wanted to leave was enraged, this time for good reasons. He and the other members of his team finally understood what it felt like to be a consumer and also what empathy, in a business environment, is all about.

The strangest thing is that most companies have never

done anything like this before. Sure, they do customer surveys. They do focus groups. But sitting down to talk to the people who actually buy and use their products or services — to understand the world from their point of view? What would be the point of that? The answer, of course, is *everything*. By bringing together employees with consumers, a company's muscle memory weakens — and resets toward a genuine customer-oriented mindset.

Until I brought employees into consumers' homes, for example, no one at Swiss International Air Lines, including the pilots and the flight crew, had ever stopped to imagine what flying might be like for their passengers. Flying was their job, what they were trained for. It was the safest, least stressful, most convenient way for them to travel from point A to point B. Thanks to employee perks, discounts, and privileges, only a few employees at Swiss International Air Lines ever have to stand in a long line to board, or worry about room in the overhead storage compartments for their carry-ons or whether they'll be able to find ground transportation when the plane lands. What was there to be worried about?

All you have to do is ask your customers — and they'll tell you everything you need to know. Last year, for example, I was consulting with a major Middle Eastern mall operator. Women are by far the largest audience in malls worldwide, so why weren't women shopping at this one? "Why don't we ask them?" I said. Oh. Right. Okay.

We interviewed a dozen or so female shoppers. They all had the same concerns. They didn't feel safe using the mall elevators, especially at night. They didn't like the layout of the parking lot. The lines separating the cars were too close together, which made parking a challenge. Three months later, mall management had installed closed-circuit television monitors in all the elevators and painted double lines between cars in the parking lots. Female mall attendance was up sharply.

The common-sense value of bringing company employees together with consumers doesn't just come from the insights gleaned by management. It also sends a signal to everyone in the organization that if senior management is willing to sit down with its customers, the company is serious about change. It's the least you need to know when you embark on a corporate transformation project.

I'm tired, you're tired. Why don't we check into a hotel?

The Dorchester Collection is made up of nine luxury hotels scattered around the world. In Los Angeles, there's the Beverly Hills Hotel and the Hotel Bel-Air. In London, there's the Dorchester Hotel, and another hotel some hundred feet away, at 45 Park Lane. A short drive from London, in Ascot, there's the Coworth Park, a Georgian manor house where Princes William and Harry stayed before Harry's wedding to Meghan Markle. In Paris, the Dorchester Collection owns Le Meurice and the Hôtel Plaza Athénée. In Rome, there's the Hotel Eden, and in Milan, the Hotel Principe di Savoia.

Just before the pandemic, the chain hired me to help it differentiate its suites from its competitors', in a world where "suite," as a concept, had pretty much lost its distinctive meaning. Less officially, my job was to retrain the people who worked in the chain's nine hotels to start seeing the world through the eyes of their guests.

It wouldn't be easy or straightforward. There's a big economic disparity between hotel employees and guests who have the wherewithal to stay at a Dorchester Collection hotel. There was also no reason to expect that a housekeeper or reception desk clerk could understand — or empathize with — the needs of a foreign dignitary, a global businessman, a tech billionaire, or a movie star.

Treat others as you would like to be treated. Such a simple concept, so why is it such an anomaly in so many companies? It always surprises me, though it probably shouldn't, considering that our best experiences as consumers — the ones we actually remember — come when a caring, considerate employee goes beyond what we anticipated or expected.

An amazing service experience similar to the one I had at the Dubai airport took place at the Beverly Hills Hotel. When I checked in, I had the beginnings of a cold — watery eyes and a hoarse voice. (No, it wasn't COVID.) Five minutes later I opened the door to my room to find that room service had already come and gone. Beside my bed was a pot of hot tea, with honey and lemon, and a handwritten note from the general manager with the name and phone number of a local doctor and a pharmacy that would deliver whatever medications I might need.

(This special treatment wasn't just for me, either. The Dorchester Collection routinely goes the extra step for *all* their guests.) Why? Because if employees were in my shoes, they would want to be treated the same way.

The reason why you and I remember experiences like these so vividly is because they're so rare — or perhaps because only rarely are we publicly in need of assistance. Most companies, hotels included, are so straitjacketed by so many systems, processes, and procedures that common sense ends up being the exception, not the rule. In the high-end hospitality industry, hotel operations work minute-by-minute and sometimes second-by-second. The problem, of course, is that a company's systems, processes, and procedures typically blind employees to who their customers are and what they want. For example, I don't think I've ever come across an operations manual with the heading DANISH GUESTS WHO MAY BE COMING DOWN WITH A COLD, just as I would never expect a hotel employee to notice my watery eyes or raspy voice. (I was amazed someone did.)

But let's imagine my cold *was* someone's responsibility. Whose would it be? The doorman's? The front office manager's? The concierge's? The bellboy's? Housekeeping's? The operations team's? The general manager's?

Along with perpetually trying to keep customers at a distance, systems and procedures have another disadvantage. They turn a company's focus inward. Along the way, continuity is lost. In Hollywood films, continuity is the process that guarantees that the smallest details of a scene remain the same, from shot to shot, even if those scenes were filmed six weeks or six months apart. Is Cary Grant wearing the same suit he had on when he entered the room, or is his necktie missing? Is the dog still asleep by the fire – and if not, where did the dog go? Continuity creates an unbroken dream of great service.

At a hotel (or any company), the role of the employees isn't just to carry out their functions but to create continuity by collaborating closely with all the other departments. I know, easier said than done, and today I'd claim that around 95 percent of all companies forget this simple, essential insight. But consistency and continuity build trust – and if there's one thing we lack in a world swimming with disinformation, it's trust. And indeed, trust usually goes hand-in-hand with common sense.

A typical hotel has lots of different departments, and only rarely do they communicate as they should. Staff turnover is high. Schedules don't always mesh. One team might work evenings, only to be replaced by another that starts work at 7 a.m. If a nighttime employee has been overseeing a guest with a migraine, will he remember to tell the team that comes on duty at 7 a.m., so it can follow up? Then there's the simple fact that hospitality jobs vary so dramatically. The livelihood of some employees – doormen, porters, bellmen – depends heavily on tips. For back-office employees, and executives, tipping isn't an issue. Hotels also have to factor in those unpredictable periods when everything happens at the same time. Half a dozen guests arrive or check out at once, and thirteen others request room service when only two employees are working the kitchen. An average hotel guest interacts indirectly with anywhere from 75 to 125 employees – reservations and booking clerks, room service, members of the housekeeping staff, and so on. An ecosystem this delicate and this sprawling requires a close interdependence among departments, a seamless continuity that doesn't happen as often as it should.

Again, one of the first steps in restoring common sense in any organization is to train employees to see the world not from the inside out, but from the outside in. One good way to initiate that is by asking employees to remember their own worst guest experiences at a hotel. We *all* have one.

Imagine that you've just flown into Los Angeles from Europe. Nonstop. A ten-to-twelve-hour flight. Two out-of-order toilets. A baby screaming like a macaw. The screen across from your seat freezing every time the pilot breaks in to describe the landscape on the left side of the plane (you're seated on the right, naturally, just as you're seated on the left whenever the best views of Paris, London, Lake Erie, or the Rockies appear on the right).

When you finally get to the hotel, you're a wreck.

It's simply not possible to feel more jetlagged than you do. You feel like a bird that's just slammed into a bay window—stunned, stale, infantile, and in an inexplicable bad temper, not to mention the fact that you *really* have to go to the bathroom. For the past few hours, you've been thinking about only one thing: the moment when you close the door to your hotel room, take off all your clothes, slip under the covers, and fall asleep.

You make polite conversation with the receptionist. She finally hands you your room card, and a masked bellman takes you upstairs. More small talk. *How was your flight? Can't complain about this weather, right? Is this your first time with us?* Being a bellman isn't an easy gig, and, as noted, he relies on tips to make a living—but you would name him a beneficiary in your will if he would just stop talking and leave. He won't, though.

His monologue, in fact, lasts—no kidding—fifteen minutes. First, he explains how to open and close your door, going into detail about the dynamics of the keycard and the key slot, and how many seconds your card should remain in the slot before you take it out. He tells you about the minibar and everything inside it. He turns the TV on and off, and shows you how to access Netflix on the remote control. By now your eyes are slits. You feel like crying or laughing hysterically. You still need to use the bathroom, badly, but your compromised brain can't find a way to put the request into words.

The bellman is telling you about the triple cleaning procedures that housekeeping carries out in every room. "That sounds so healthy," you say, you hope conclusively, but he's not close to being done. He's now moved on to the hotel's award-winning "pillow menu," and the feather content inside each of the six pillow models. *Please suffocate me with a pillow right now*, you want to say. Wait, did you actually say that, or just think it? You're so out of it you can't tell. What's left of your brain clears long enough for you to register that he's over by the safe now, telling you how to set the combination.

You tip him generously, to force him to leave, but it appears you may have overtipped since your generosity ignites even more conversational embers. Do you know about the hotel's award-winning farm-to-table restaurant? The tomatoes and red onions are from an organic farm outside Napa, the beef is flown in from Japan, and the chef makes her own gelato. "Hey—I've kept you long enough," you say, summoning the deflective charm of the grandmother you never had.

When he's gone, you double-bolt the door and stagger into the bathroom. Afterward, you feel better. Not a lot, but enough so that for the first time you notice the colorful garden four stories below you. Deprived of fresh air during your flight, you decide to open the windows. But they won't open. They *can't* open. There's no latch. There's not even a windowsill. Why? Aware of your weird rage coming back, you tell yourself that a long cooling shower might be in order. Unfortunately, housekeeping forgot to return the shower nozzle to its vertical position, and a firehose of the coldest water you've ever felt jets into your face, soaking you and your clothes, and almost knocking you to the ground.

The doorbell rings. It's your luggage. The masked porter, who has no idea that the bellman has already told you about the room's many amenities, starts to tell you how to access the TV's premium channels. Aware that the minibar, the safe, and the feather content of the pillows in the hotel's award-winning pillow menu are up next, you tip him, and he leaves. With your room and wallet now empty, you take off your clothes, slide under the covers, and fall asleep.

Halfway through your dream, the combination alarm clock–iPhone charger on the far side of the bed starts playing Phil Collins's "Sussudio." The last person who stayed in this room must have set the alarm for 4:40 p.m., and evidently housekeeping forgot to reset it. *Su-su-su-dio-oh-oh.* You can't figure out which button turns it off — *Oh, give me a chance, give me a sign-n-n-n* — so you end up ripping the plug out of the wall, along with a few crumbs of plaster.

You fall asleep again, but you're awoken again by another knock. Minibar check. You fall asleep again. Another knock. Room check. (Why? Is the room going anywhere? Has it been stolen?) You fall back asleep. Another knock. Housekeeping. Stomping outside, you jam the DO NOT DISTURB sign over the knob, slamming the door behind you. You fall asleep yet again. The phone rings. Housekeeping. They noticed you put the DO NOT DISTURB sign on your door, so instead of knocking, and bothering you, they're calling instead: Do you want turn-down service tonight?

Your grievances only multiply as the week goes on.

For example, there's the two-day-old glass of red wine you didn't entirely finish. Instead of removing it, housekeeping covered the top with some kind of frilly white — what would you call it? — "paperlet." This signals that yes, they saw the glass, but they assume you're not quite done with it, even though the wine looks like a patch of dried blood, and a family of gnats are whizzing around the rim. Maybe you're testing out an important new theory involving fruit flies and genetics? For heaven's sake, why don't they just take the damn thing away? Well, fifty years ago no doubt, a guest probably got mad when

You know those thumb-size shampoo and conditioner bottles in the shower? Why is the writing on them so small? You can't tell which one is which unless you have your glasses on, and who wears their glasses in the shower?

housekeeping took away his half-drunk glass of flat ginger ale, so from the hotel's perspective, it's probably better to err on the side of caution. Something similar probably explains why none of the hotel windows open. A guest probably tried to climb up onto the roof back in 1947, inspiring the hotel to seal the glass in place to prevent the possibility of any lawsuits.

You know those thumb-size shampoo and conditioner bottles in the shower? Why is the writing on them so small? You can't tell which one is which unless you have your glasses on, and who wears their glasses in the shower?

Remember your first night? Instead of going around extinguishing every lamp, you shut off the room's "master switch." No one told you that doing that kills the electricity in all the wall outlets, which is why your phone, tablet, and laptop didn't charge and wouldn't turn on in the morning.

Whose idea was it to position the toilet paper roll nearly two feet behind and to the bottom right of the toilet? A performance artist's? An octopus's? To reach even one sheet, you separated your shoulder while torquing your wrist in a nature-defying way you've seen only in sports injury videos that come with the warning: MAY BE UPSETTING TO SOME VIEWERS.

Was the U.S. Army Corps of Engineers responsible for making your bed? It's impossible to slip under the covers in any kind of lighthearted slumber-party way. The sheets and blankets are stretched so tightly, so packed in, it feels like someone glue-gunned them to the mattress. You feel like a form letter trying to jam yourself inside an envelope. Once you manage to get under, you're pinned there like a dead butterfly in some crazy person's insect album. Kicking one foot out the first night, you heard a terrifying ripping sound that made you worry you'd broken the bed.

These and other service issues typically faced by travelers underscore an important common-sense consideration that few at the Dorchester Collection had ever really thought about, namely, *What state of mind are guests in when they arrive at a hotel?*

The answer of course varies, but in general, guests who check in are thoroughly exhausted and jetlagged. They don't want to talk to the reception clerk, the bellman, the porter, or anybody. They just want to go to sleep. That's why one of the first exercises I do with hotel employees around the world is ask them to simulate how guests *feel*. In the case of the Dorchester, how could employees optimize the "consumer journey" from the moment guests check in to the moment they check out? Staffers reconnect with common sense not just when they're able to imagine what consumers are experiencing but when they *live* those experiences themselves. An experiment I did several years ago with one of the big credit card companies illustrates this point pretty clearly.

One of the (many) customer service issues the company was up against was that, well, its customers flat out *hated* it. They shared that loathing on Facebook and Twitter, and left horrible reviews online. It was unanimous: the credit card company's customer service was a disaster. The wait times were interminable. When you finally got an operator on the line, she would transfer you from one department to the next, eating up an hour of your day. For their part, credit card executives had no sympathy whatsoever for customers. They were simply numbers on an Excel sheet, that's all. The most they were willing to do to placate them was to initiate a new loyalty program.

Observing this dynamic, I thought up a small experiment. It would require secrecy and take some legwork, but if it worked it might give credit card executives the opportunity to see the world from a customer's point of view. First, I made a dinner reservation for the team and me at a restaurant, but not before asking employees in the fraud division to make sure their bosses' credit cards wouldn't work for the next twenty-four hours. That night, we all piled into a taxi and headed out to eat.

> If my secret experiment worked — canceling all their credit cards without them knowing it — credit card executives might have the opportunity to see the world from a customer's point of view.

When we arrived, one of the managers gave the driver his credit card to pay the fare. Of course, it was rejected. He then had to call the company — *the company where he worked* — to figure out why. It took a long time to get through. *Call volume is unexpectedly high right now*, said the robot-woman. *Our customer service representatives are busy helping other callers. Please hold on for the next available operator. We appreciate your patience. Your call may be recorded for training purposes.* Then, as if addressing a dimwitted child, *Did you know you can also access your account online? Just type in www . . .*

The manager waited. And waited some more. Canned music, heavy on the strings, helped pass the time. *Your call is important to us*, the robot-woman assured him now and then. *Please remain on the line.* The cheesy music started up again. At one point, the poor guy was asked to press 9. Then 5. Then 7. Another fifteen minutes of his life went by. By the time the call ended, he was in the foulest mood possible. Over and over again, he announced just how much he hated — *hated* — the credit card company. "Would a loyalty program make things better for you?" I asked. "You must be *nuts!*" he said. It was then I admitted I'd set the whole thing up.

His expression, in that moment, gave everything away. The only way he could possibly understand the pain his own customers went through was by experiencing that pain himself. Ten years of field reports, pages of endless statistics, and focus groups had had no effect on him. Finally, he was able to empathize with the people who used his product and service.

The team and I spent the rest of the night analyzing customer data. Every year, 23 percent of all credit card customers went through a similar experience. A lost, stolen, or hacked card. Fraudulent charges. Identity theft. A card rejected by the bank for no apparent reason. A few months later, the credit card company had completely restructured their customer service department to align with what their *customers* wanted.

In some situations, of course, experiencing a customer's pain just isn't possible, not firsthand. You can only imagine it. Picture, for a moment, how you might feel if you were in my friend Lee's shoes. Lee has been a sleepwalker since he was a boy. At home, at friend's houses, in hotels — it doesn't matter. Given this disorder, it's probably not the best idea for him to sleep in the nude, but there you have it. A few years ago, Lee booked a room at a fancy new West Coast hotel with glass elevators, glass railings — glass everything. Sometime during the night, he awoke and, not aware he was sleepwalking, opened the door from his room and went out into the hallway.

The door clicked shut behind him, locking him out. It was at that point that Lee woke up. It was 3:10 in the morning. There was no phone in the hallway, and his own cell was recharging in his room. He was completely naked. With no other options, he boarded the glass elevator and pressed L for Lobby. When the doors opened, he snaked his head out. *Psst!* Lee hissed. No response. *Psst!* Lee hissed again. Finally, the guy at reception looked up to see a disembodied male head sticking out of the elevator.

When he investigated, he found Lee, huddled in one corner, with both hands shielding himself, like in those Renaissance paintings of Adam and Eve. Lee explained what had happened and that he was locked out of his room; could he please get a replacement key? "I'm sorry," the clerk said, "but I can't supply you with a duplicate key unless you show some proof of your identity — a driver's license or a passport." "I don't have any ID on me right this second!" Lee said. "I'm sorry," the employee said, "it's strict company policy."

After a heated back-and-forth discussion and the temporary loan of a towel, the desk clerk, now joined by a security guard, accompanied Lee upstairs. The guard unlocked the door, and flanked by both men, Lee unlocked the room safe, took out his passport, and was able to show proof that, yes, he was who he said he was and in fact now had no secrets at all. From anybody.

"Force majeure" isn't an expression you hear much these days. Known elsewhere as an "act of God," "force majeure" refers to an unforeseen situation, or event, that prevents something that was scheduled from taking place. The COVID-19 pandemic, the flat tire that makes you late for a party, the snowstorm that keeps you from going to work—those are real-life force majeure excuses. I had no idea how familiar I'd become with the concept of force majeure when I started working for Maersk, the huge international shipping company.

Along with Lego, Maersk is probably the most prominent, admired, and successful company in Danish history. Founded in 1904 and headquartered in Copenhagen, Maersk is the world's largest supply vessel container ship company in both fleet size and cargo capacity, with 343 different ports in 121 countries. Maersk basically *invented* modern-day shipping, and today ships one-fifth of all the goods on this planet. The average Maersk vessel has room for 18,000 twenty-foot-long containers, which hold more than 150,000 tons of materials. It could be 8,000 BMWs or millions of Nike sneakers, shorts, and tank tops or every species of flower that will be sold in Nigeria for the next month or thousands of tons of pharmaceuticals, grain and soybean meal, or pesticides.

As the largest player in the international shipping industry for more than a century, Maersk, I soon found out, was an extraordinarily rational, left-brained company. Not surprisingly Maersk's IT system was cutting-edge as well.

So why had the company called me in, and how could I help them improve their culture and business?

Understand, first, that shipping and transport is the world's oldest commercial industry. Its systems, practices, and operations have worked well since the early twentieth century. Those enormous containers you see inside shipping vessels? Maersk *invented* them. But as the decades passed and Maersk became a publicly traded company, shareholder pressure led to increased optimization of every aspect of the company's business. Not surprisingly, Maersk began focusing exclusively on its upcoming quarterly report. Which was totally fine . . . until share prices began falling. Departments started pointing fingers at other departments. Meanwhile, employees were scared of what would happen if they didn't hit their KPIs. Maersk *knew* it had to change somehow, but at the same time, it feared what might happen if it *did* change.

A customer-centric business should be designed less around what a *company* wants than around what its *customers* want. What was the best way to infuse this crucial perspective into a company with 88,000 employees? In such a big organization, it's important to start small, which is why I focused my attention on improving customer service in China, India, and Germany, three of Maersk's key markets. If, together, we could turn those three around, senior management would know we were on the right track.

My colleagues and I flew to Shanghai and began interviewing Maersk call center employees. No one really knew
why customer satisfaction at Maersk was lower than it should
be. The employees told me they were just doing their jobs,
servicing their customers and the company to the best of their
abilities. I took a seat, put on a headset, and, with the help of a
translator, began listening in to one call after another.

At first nothing seemed out of the ordinary. A customer
would call in and lodge a complaint or describe their predic-
ament. Noting the issue, call center employees then tried to
solve it, and if they couldn't, they forwarded the call to another division that could. Again, nothing unusual, but when
we later analyzed call center data, I was struck not only by
the sheer number and pace of incoming calls, but by the fact
that many calls were filed under the category Force Majeure.
I wondered: How could so many transatlantic shipping problems be caused by divine interference? Was it Poseidon? A
few days later, I discovered that Force Majeure had less to do
with vengeful deities and more to do with an unrealistic set
of KPIs.

You see, when Maersk call center employees clicked on the
FORCE MAJEURE button, they had to fill out only one page of
notes. But for all other issues or complaints, they were obliged
to fill out four or five pages. At roughly a minute a page, that
meant that their days could be eaten up in one five-minute
increment after another. In short, clicking FORCE MAJEURE
saved time.

How had this been allowed to happen? The short answer
is silos and KPIs. Performance and productivity in Maersk's
call centers wasn't measured on state-of-the-art customer
service but rather on a single metric: *time*. This explained the

almost frantic productivity of call center employees. How fast could they resolve a caller's question before moving on to the next customer, and the one after that? That was the key.

Not only was the FORCE MAJEURE button a way for employees to keep pace with department KPIs, I found out about another trick that was used by one of Maersk's biggest competitors: the BLIND FORWARD button. This one falls into the category of *anti*-customer service. It's practically the definition of "passive-aggressive." The BLIND FORWARD button is a way to deal with a customer who calls in with a problem you have no idea how to solve or who maybe you find annoying or long-winded. By pressing the BLIND FORWARD button, instead of solving the problem, the caller is randomly transferred to another person or department in the company—sales, marketing, operations, or IT. A customer soon finds himself talking to a totally confused and unprepared employee who has no idea why his phone rang or how to respond. I can't help but wonder whether the BLIND FORWARD button exists just to torment customers, and also how widespread it might be in other industries!

A few months later, common sense had been restored. Maersk management changed the KPIs in their call centers to measure the essential qualities that led to actual customer satisfaction—reliability, issue resolution, and invoice quality. These were small, unsexy changes to be sure, but once they were made, customer satisfaction nearly doubled, and to my mind, clients were decidedly less likely to reach out to Maersk's growing list of competitors.

But as far as common sense is concerned, who wins with the BLIND FORWARD button? The company? Consumers? Anybody?

• • •

As noted, most positive common-sense changes that improve customer experience are fairly simple to figure out. All companies have to do is simply take the time to talk to their own customers.

For example, why did Cath Kidston wallets sell well in the United Kingdom, but not in Asia, the company's second biggest market? I posed this question to nearly a dozen Japanese consumers and quickly found out why.

In the West, wallets come in a predictable, uniform size, with a ridge of compartments designed to fit various forms of ID, debit, credit, membership, library, or business cards. These cards also come in a relatively uniform size, and wallet manufacturers design their products accordingly. So why weren't Cath Kidston wallets selling in Asia? Well, generally speaking, the Japanese carry many more cards in their wallets than Westerners do. Japanese cards are also smaller on average than Western cards and come in an odd array of different sizes. Very simply, it was a matter of fit. Beyond the sheer volume of cards that most Japanese people carry with them, half of them are either too large or too small for a Cath Kidston wallet.

In hindsight, shouldn't the company have picked up on this before releasing wallets in Asia? Also, why wasn't the company paying closer attention to what went on in its own retail stores? Let me explain: If mothers with daughters were among Cath's biggest customers, why were all the store mannequins of women in their thirties and forties? Wouldn't it make more sense to pose a smaller female mannequin beside her mother and attire her in more youthful clothes? For many women, the mother-daughter matrix is a snapshot of an ideal family, one where the two dress alike, never argue, and tell each other everything — never mind the reality, but fashion, as everyone knows, markets an ideal — as well as one where a mother can pass her own traditions and tastes to the next generation. When store managers began posing girl mannequins next to woman mannequins, sales of Cath Kidston's more junior clothing lines went up immediately.

Last but not least, women who shopped in Cath Kidston stores often found themselves buying so many items they couldn't hold them all in their hands. When that happened, they returned some of the items to the shelves. I suggested that Cath Kidston stores provide shopping baskets, which almost immediately led to higher profits in stores. But what about men, who often accompanied their wives and girlfriends, most of the time reluctantly? It's hard to keep a partner waiting, especially in a store devoted exclusively to female tastes. So we created and installed "parking spots" for men. Seats can go a long way toward making men — grown men, teenaged men, any kind of men — cool their jets. Perhaps not a big deal, but for their customers, it certainly made for a more pleasant excursion into the stores. Again, just an application of a little common sense.

4

POLITICS: THE INVISIBLE STRAITJACKET

MY FIRST REAL JOB WAS WORKING at an advertising agency in Skive, a small, rural town in Denmark. I was young, energetic, and crackling with ideas and convictions. I was also naive, though naive people don't usually think of themselves as such, which just adds in another layer of naiveté. Mostly, I remember myself as being incredibly driven and ambitious. I also had the ear of the agency's CEO who, if I remember right, saw me as a hypercharged version of his younger self.

A few months after starting, I felt comfortably settled. I was one of the gang. In no way did I suspect what was really going on behind the curtain.

One of my coworkers was an older female senior art director. She had the office next to mine and was close friends with a senior consultant, a fellow in his late fifties whose office was down the hall. Often, I saw the two of them in conversation or coming back from lunch. Nothing romantic, just two colleagues who'd been with the agency for a while and who looked out for each other — more than I knew, as it turned out.

About nine months after starting work there, I got to the office early one morning, as was my habit. The senior art director's door was closed. This was a little strange, but it became even stranger as the morning wore on. There was a steady stream of people — mostly colleagues of mine — going in and out of her office. I finally asked one of them what was going on. "I was just in there being interviewed about *you*," she said. "She was asking me *a lot* of questions."

Me? What *about* me? Had I done something wrong? If so, what? Why would anyone take the trouble to interview my coworkers about *me?* Somewhat awkwardly, my colleague told me she got the strong sense that the senior art director disliked me. Okay, she *hated* me. She seemed to be lining up a coalition to get me fired from the agency.

"But they can't do that!" I said. I felt hurt, confused, and, above all, outraged. Could "they" do that? Who were "they" anyway? Until then I felt I'd done everything right. Attend school. Do well. Study hard. Ace papers and tests. Open my own advertising agency at age twelve. Get a job. Work crazy hours. Follow whatever rules were worth following and challenge the ones that felt stale or stupid. Nothing my colleague was telling me now fit into this narrative.

But all of it was true. Later it was confirmed that the senior art director had instigated a small, ferocious whispering campaign against me. Her goal was to convince as many colleagues as possible to get me fired, to protect the job of her close friend, the senior consultant.

And the truth was, not *once* had I ever thought about someday taking over his job! Was I so blindly, irrationally

A political company is one where management and employees are so preoccupied by their own divisions, hierarchies, and metrics that they lose sight of anything outside themselves — including their customers.

driven that I couldn't see that if I kept doing what I was doing, I might be next in line to succeed him? It was my first, but not my last, experience with company politics. A few years later, strangely enough, the situation was reversed. I was working for BBDO, the global advertising agency. I had an older assistant. Walking past her desk one afternoon, I couldn't help noticing her screen saver. A tiny, happy, carefree panda bear was bouncing up and down into a starless sky. How adorable was that? Then I noticed the tiny panda bear had a ball and chain attached to its right ankle. "What's that?" I asked, pointing at the screen. "Oh," my assistant said casually, "that's *me* working for *you*."

I was put on notice, to say the least. I'd never thought of myself as a punitive or demanding person to work for, someone who sucked the joy out of panda bears. Was I *that* much of a misery as a boss? Without even being aware of it, I'd created my own little ring of politics.

When I point the finger at corporate politics for helping to contribute to the erosion of common sense in the workplace, I'm talking about something subtler, more indefinite and harder to decipher. As my own experiences attest, the nature of corporate politics can often insidiously grow and ruin relationships and productivity without your being aware of it.

Whenever status, power, ambition, and competitiveness come together, politics rears up. It's human nature, *animal* nature, and as rife in the business world as it was back in high school. A political company is one where management and employees are so preoccupied by their own divisions, hierarchies, and metrics that they lose sight of anything outside themselves. In fact, probably the best way to understand politics in organizations is by picturing an unconventional game of chess.

I want you to imagine two players seated opposite each other, a chessboard between them. At first nothing seems off. There are thirty-two black and white chess pieces in all, sixteen per player. As any chess player knows, the goal of the game is to checkmate—that is to say, entrap, frustrate, or neutralize—your opponent's king by strategically advancing a combination of your pawns, rooks, bishops, knights, and so on. Chess rules allow some pieces to move one space, others two. Still others move on a diagonal. Navigating company politics is a lot like playing chess, the core difference being your opponent has decided to bend the rules. He's actually *disguised* all his pieces, meaning that nothing is as it seems. The queen resembles a bishop. The knight looks like a queen. The pawns and the rooks have switched places. The rules no longer apply. Do you move one space, two spaces, or diagonally? Is the king in charge, is the bishop calling the shots, and what role does the queen play?

Figuring out who's *really* in charge in an organization is like that. That's why the first thing I do when I start working for a company is sit down and interview employees.

Along with an official organizational chart, businesses also have an unofficial org chart, one that really reveals what's going on in the company. Studies back this up. In one, a munitions plant received a contract requiring employees to increase production to fifty units per day. Industrial engineers came in, new staff was hired, the plant manager was replaced, the production line was expanded. It didn't make any difference. The plant was stuck at thirty-five units per day. An outside engineer was brought aboard to see what was really going on.

Instead of going around measuring things, the engineer hung out, watched, took notes, and even went out drinking with employees. He soon learned that despite what the "official" org chart proclaimed, the *real* power in the company lay with a well-respected, powerful, somewhat fearsome female veteran. Unhappy with the way management had treated her once and highly protective of her workers, she controlled the speed of production. In this case, she wasn't about to let the company increase production to fifty units per day. The engineer sat down with her, listened to her complaints, explained how the new contract benefited her employees – and before long the company's production met, and sometimes exceeded, its new goals.

Then there's Nortel. The huge telecom company was growing fast, and in response the company hired numerous new staffers at all levels. They all knew the official org chart cold. But so what? The problem was that no one was able or empowered to make decisions. As a result, despite its growth, Nortel turned into one big bottleneck. It began losing ground to more agile rivals and ultimately filed for bankruptcy. No one there had a clue about the so-called unofficial org chart or that *that* was the one they should be focusing on.

Think about your own company. Are there a bunch of unspoken rules, ones written in invisible ink? Are you *expected* to work on weekends or make an appearance at the weekly Friday meeting, even though no one explicitly says so, but if you blow it off, everyone will consider you something less than a team player? Is there a certain brand of car you're expected to drive or wristwatch you should avoid wearing simply because your boss has a cheaper model? Does HR call the shots, even though no one really talks about it or likes to admit it?

Knowing all this, I typically interview a representative sample of everyone in the organization – top management, middle management, junior employees, interns, receptionists, and sometimes even members of the cleaning crew. I map out email and phone flows. With employees' consent, I even study the message chains on WhatsApp, the private voice-messaging platform. On WhatsApp I might find that a group in one department is having an intense conversation with another employee group, despite those two groups having no obvious connection, well, at least if the org chart is to be believed. *If you have a problem, who in the company would you go to?* I ask employees. *Where do ideas in this company get killed? And who are the five people here who really make your life difficult?*

I might find, for instance, that the CEO defers all decisions to the head of HR; that a company's operational director is a simmering troublemaker who's only interested in preserving power, discouraging collaboration, and undermining her colleagues; or that it's the grumpy guy working in legal on the fourth floor who historically kills every consulting project. I also hear positive stuff too – for example, the names of the three employees who can make things happen or who

Navigating company politics is a lot like playing chess, the core difference being your opponent has decided to bend the rules, so that nothing is as it seems. Is the king in charge, is the bishop calling the shots, and what role does the queen play?

add a fresh twist to any problem. (Whenever I share this information with CEOs, their response is usually, "My God, it took me a *year* to find that out.")

In the wake of the 2008 recession, Warren Buffett was quoted as saying, "You only find out who is swimming naked when the tide goes out." Something similar happens when a company's unofficial org chart is revealed. More than a placid postcard portrait of an ocean, you suddenly become aware of tide pools, sandbars, seagrass, and scraggly underwater life. You notice the rust on the buoys, the husk of a drowned ketch, and the rip currents that can easily drag employees out to sea.

Who are the sneakiest political players in organizations? Well, Hollywood films often feature young, ambitious employees with rotted souls who stop at nothing to reach the top of their profession. When the movie ends, they stand alone in huge, magnificent glass offices, gazing down at the city landscape below. *Was it all worth it? I'm a lying sociopathic narcissist with no friends.* (Many in the audience sit there, thinking, *Yup — totally worth it,* but on their way out of the theater, whisper to their companions, *That ending was so devastating, how alone that person was.*) Fortunately, I've never met anyone like that in real life. There are countless good, smart, compassionate, well-meaning people in companies — I would describe most of them that way, in fact. But put them all together and, more likely than not, your business will start to feel like Congress. Here a few warning signs:

MULTIPLE LEVELS

The most successful companies in the world have the fewest reporting levels. Three, maybe, at most four. In companies with up to a dozen reporting levels (I know of one company that has eighteen!), politics increases accordingly and, inevitably, so does the workload. For every reporting layer, you can add another 10 percent to that workload. If there are five levels, that's 10 percent *plus* 10 percent *on top of* 10 percent, and up and up it goes. In some companies, roughly 60 percent of employees' time is squandered on reporting levels, quashing if not eradicating real employee productivity.

SCATTERED GEOGRAPHY

Imagine that your company has offices in New York, Los Angeles, Amsterdam, London, Singapore, Mumbai, and the lost continent of Atlantis. This means that along with doing business, you will most likely have issues around language and, relatedly, education. You will encounter issues around differing cultures and reference points. Issues around time zones. Issues around varying seniority levels. Add to which when you communicate with an office 5,000 miles away, it's usually done via Skype. You can just imagine the amount of confusion, most of it unbridgeable, that comes as a result.

Of all these, language is probably the most important, and divisive. A company's workforce is a tribe fluent in its own language and vocabulary, made up of shorthand words and acronyms that puzzle and exclude most outsiders. Either you're an Us or a Them, a member of the in-crowd or an outcast. How can a global organization with offices all over the world possibly create a shared language that transcends local affiliations? A shared language is a genuine point of differentiation for a company — and it's where many of them fall short.

FLIP-FLOPPING BOSSES

I wrote earlier that most leaders will tell you that common-sense issues in their company are minimal. Similarly, most bosses will tell you that once they've made up their mind, that's all there is to that. Yet employees usually have a different take and will swear that their bosses are all over the place. Typically this is because bosses often give latitude to employees to make their own decisions, and employees will end up doing something that their bosses wanted to hear.

A HOMOGENOUS EMPLOYEE BASE

Hey, I get it. If you're a company like Maersk, the last thing you want is to hire a bunch of ceramicists and slam poets. Instead, you focus on employees who have a bias toward extreme left-brain thinking. With its reputation for dizzyingly difficult interview questions, Google is the same way. Until recently, the questions its staff asked potential hires included, "Model raindrops falling on a sidewalk (sidewalk is 1 meter, and raindrops are 1 centimeter). How could we know when the sidewalk is completely wet?" and of course the easy-to-answer, "How many haircuts do you think happen in America every year?"

But I can almost guarantee you that nine times out of ten, a company with a homogenous employee base has minimal politics. Everyone gets along pretty well, even if common sense and empathy barely exist. But if any disruption happens, the company's internal resistance — what I like to call its immune system — erupts, rejecting the alien intruder, and politics settles over the organization like a fine ash. The sad news, however, is that in today's world, disruption is a stable inventory item on every company's agenda.

SILOS AND KPIS

Let's talk about KPIs and corporate common sense.

The average company has between 50 and 150 KPIs. Forget the aspirational idea that the sum is always greater than the parts. The hysterical multiplication of KPIs means that many organizations today are comprised *only* of separate parts. I've seen numerous companies whose KPIs include "customer focus" or "customer satisfaction." These KPIs are very real — but on closer inspection I find the company is allocating only 1 or 2 percent of its focus to this metric. How can a company be 2 percent customer-focused? That comes out to only three days of customer focus per year!

Even worse, the proliferation of KPIs often has a peculiarly sorry consequence: employees, and silos, become so narrow-minded it seldom occurs to anyone to think holistically. In one company I consulted for, a few older employees told me that before KPIs multiplied, they were proud to say they knew every customer's name. But as time went on, Joe and Irene turned into Customer 1129 and Customer 3094. Swapping names for numbers is as good a metaphor as any for companies that are inadvertently severing connections with the very people they're supposed to serve.

Prompted by the demands of Wall Street as investors focus more on next quarter's performance results than on the CEO's long-term vision, KPIs today are symbolic of a rush and drive for "clarity" and "accountability" across organizations. Sure, KPIs provide both those things, but they can do so at the expense of cohesion and culture. The result? Narrow-minded paralysis, which in turn prompts the need for even *more* metrics, summaries, proxies, reports, and presentations.

Politics in companies, like any smokescreen, is the enemy of common sense. When company dynamics and priorities are unclear, not only does the resulting confusion mess up the chain of command but inevitably companies often privilege personalities over principles. Organizations pivot inward. The more inward-focused and preoccupied a company becomes, the less it sees itself with any real objectivity or clarity. It's like an invisible straightjacket. An alternate reality soon becomes unofficial law. In this climate, a company can pretend that an utterly irrational decision was made *only* after serious thought and analysis. As a result, common sense gets pushed off to the side.

For example, early on in my career, I used to fly SAS business class a lot. One day I boarded a flight and instead of the usual hot meal, the airline served . . . air. Okay, a small baggie of something or other containing *mostly* air. When I asked the flight attendant why, he told me that SAS had carried out a comprehensive study, asking more than 1,000 passengers whether they preferred a hot meal or no meal. The respondents who voted for no meal won by a huge margin.

Where was the common sense? In a world where most airliners offer passengers a bag of pretzels the size of a cricket's purse, who could possibly get behind a rule permanently banning hot meals on a plane? When was this "comprehensive study" carried out? What time of day? Were the respondents all drunk? I imagine the study was carried out using the following wording: *If you could save $500 on your flight from Copenhagen to Stockholm, in exchange for no hot meal service in the cabin, would you choose a $500 discount or a reheated meal?* Skewed, manipulative studies such as these allow companies to wash their hands of something costly and effortful (hot meals) while enforcing a preexisting belief in the organization, all the while telling their passengers, *You spoke and we heard you!* I might add that the big consulting firms are masters at inventing reality out of context or seeing the world from only one point of view. Once a company hires them, top management lays out a hypothesis, and six months later a study is published that – wouldn't you know it – absolutely confirms that same hypothesis. For companies, it's akin to purchasing validation.

Have you ever had a conversation with a businessperson where he or she said one thing, but you know—*you know!*—he or she meant something else? Of course, degrees of indirection vary around the world. The Dutch and the Danes, for example, are known for their frankness, whereas Swedes generally seek consensus. Buried under the apologetic politeness shown by many British businesspeople is a company's hidden "kitchen cabinet," where the real decisions are made. In America, candor is discouraged. Instead of disagreeing with you or telling you your idea or strategy is flat-out terrible and will never work, businesspeople in the United States use "diplomatic" words such as "pushback" and "blowback." Have you noticed that no one ever gets fired in the United States? They "step down," like elves softly descending a step ladder, or "are let go," like a child's balloon sailing up over the trees. Then there's, "Regarding your status here, we've decided to head in a different direction," as though they're tourists who've decided to take the coastal route rather than the main highway.

Here are some others, none of which have much to do with common sense.

Phrase: *Let's park that idea.* Real meaning: *I'm not interested in you and your dumb idea. But let's both pretend I plan to revisit it in the future. Stay tuned for nothing! Maybe both of us will forget about it.*

Phrase: *Send me a deck!* Real meaning: *Go away. Once you put your dumb idea in a PowerPoint, I'll have more numbers and bullet points to justify kicking you to the curb. That is, if I ever get around to reading that PowerPoint, which I won't.*

Phrase: *Great idea! Let's put that in our existing workstream/our project group/our existing committee/our next leadership council.* Real meaning: *I'll let your idea join forces with a stale idea that two dozen people have labored on for the past seven years. I don't have to tell you that nothing will come of it!*

Phrase: *If Zoe supports it, I will too.* Real meaning: *I lack courage. If I support you, I might fail. Please don't make me fail. If Zoe supports it, at least I can have some company in my failure.*

Phrase: *Let's cancel our meeting; what's the best number to reach you on?* Real meaning: *You're in deep trouble.*

Phrase: *Instead of our phone call, why don't you email me?* Real meaning: *You're in the deepest shit possible.*

Phrase: *Martin, you have to understand something. Look, Martin, at the end of the day . . .* Real meaning: *Martin, I'm using your name every few words in conversation, Martin, in a way I hope sounds personal and loving. Martin, it's actually a way for me to soften what I'm about to tell you, which is that I hate your idea, Martin; I hate you, Martin; I even hate the <u>name</u> Martin, and I don't ever want to see you, Martin, again.*

Dissembling language aside, the real root cause of company politics is secrecy. Few things can destine a company to failure more than an absence of transparency.

I once worked for a supermarket chain in great financial distress. The company was secretive to an almost preposterous degree. This made no sense to me. Why did the organization play everything so close to the bone? Why was it so tight-lipped to the point where the president wasn't allowed to give speeches, employees couldn't post anything online, and everywhere you turned you ran up against another NDA (nondisclosure agreement)? What could anyone want to steal from a failing supermarket? A Mylar balloon? A slice of old turkey?

Then the company began to change its approach. They loosened up and became much more transparent. Later the company's CEO admitted that transparency had taught him two crucial things. First, by communicating to the rest of the world what he was doing, he was far more likely to attract better talent. Second, he realized that a general lack of transparency ended up isolating his own employees. The company's new transparency meant that suddenly everyone wanted to join forces with his supermarket and be associated with success. The company's new openness turned into a positive, self-fulfilling prophecy.

Transparency aside, what is the best way to depoliticize a company and infuse common sense into its operations?

One way companies can rid themselves of destructive politics is by actively learning how to rebound after making a major mistake. Let me cite an example. United Airlines is often cited as a company that suffered a spectacularly well-publicized browbeating, but the case is worth revisiting, not just because the company exhibited incredibly poor judgment but because the incident ended up restoring a measure of common sense to the organization.

In 2017, at Chicago's O'Hare airport, Department of Aviation security officers forcibly and physically removed a sixty-nine-year-old Vietnamese American passenger, who happened to be a doctor, from a fully booked flight. He was literally dragged off the flight by security guards. The incident came in response to United offering vouchers to four passengers who might be willing to give up their seats and take a later flight (four airline personnel needed to fly somewhere). When no one volunteered, United randomly selected four passengers for "involuntary removal." What the airliner forgot was that people like taking photos and videos, and camera phone footage can be damning.

Twenty-four hours after a video of the incident appeared on news outlets worldwide, United CEO Oscar Munoz released a statement in support of the cabin crew and the company. Airline personnel were following correct procedures, he said, adding that the passenger in question was disruptive. No one else aboard the plane went along with this character assessment, and neither did their videos.

> Most of us probably remember sitting around a campfire when we were kids. During workshops, I create my own version of one, and in countless darkened rooms, where no one can see anyone else's eyes and titles, positions, and salaries are irrelevant, employees become . . . honest.

Forty-eight hours later, Munoz reversed his position and issued an apology. The CEO ended up losing a widely anticipated promotion to company chairman, and the passenger in question settled with United for an undisclosed amount of money. More importantly, fueled by a new dose of common sense, United's culture reawakened, giving employees free rein to behave differently—and reinstall common sense—from that point onward.

In the absence of a crisis, transparency is the best way to eradicate politics and to restore a company's common sense. The best companies are trustworthy and high in emotional intelligence. They are places where secrecy is neither encouraged nor rewarded. They also tend to hire a broad variety of employees. The leaders in these companies are unafraid of hiring people smarter than they are and of elevating others, without taking credit.

One exercise I do to root out politics and to underscore common sense in companies is to build a campfire. Most of us probably remember sitting around a campfire when we were kids. It's an experience that touches every one of our senses. The heat coming from the fire. The sound of crackling kindling. The aroma of hot dogs burning and marshmallows melting. Your friends laughing, whispering, telling secrets. A study done by anthropologists at the University of Alabama found that sitting beside a campfire lowers blood pressure and reduces other stress indicators. Basically the longer we sit beside a fire, the more relaxed we become.

Now, I don't build an actual campfire inside a company. Instead, during a workshop, I turn off all the overhead lights and place some form of illumination in the center of a room. It could be a cluster of candles or even a video of a crackling campfire. In this darkened room, where no one can see anyone else's eyes and titles, positions, and salaries are irrelevant, employees start talking. They usually forget they're in a room inside an office building, forget about what's on their checklist tomorrow and the day after, forget about compliance and legal issues and regulations. Instead, they become . . . honest.

This doesn't surprise me. According to one source, campfires produce "what researchers call a 'soft fascination,' modestly grabbing our attention while allowing the analytical parts of our brain to rest. This is the 'restoration theory' of nature: nature allows the always-on, critical part of our minds to take it easy, while prodding the long-dormant, open-ended part of our minds to come alive."

Over the years I've been surprised by how many companies I've worked at have adopted my campfire concept, turning it into a regular habit. In the supermarket chain I mentioned, management has now implemented the campfire idea in every single store. Every Friday afternoon, two dozen or so employees gather to discuss problems, complaints, and issues raised that week by consumers. Needless to say, the impact of organizational politics is minimal.

Like United Airlines, Wells Fargo, the multinational institution, got into trouble back in 2016 when the bank fired more than 5,000 workers for creating millions of nonexistent accounts. The CEO left, and the bank appointed new board members and directors. You'd think that would be the end of it, but it was just the beginning. Wells Fargo's problems were pervasive. The bank charged its customers for mortgage fees that weren't merited and pushed them into getting unnecessary automobile and even *pet* insurance. More recently, a computer glitch caused numerous customers to have their homes foreclosed. Regulators sanctioned Wells Fargo. The Justice Department, the Securities and Exchange Commission, and other agencies are investigating them. Today, with its growth stalled, the bank is trying to regain the trust of its customers (and everybody else).

I can't say for sure, but I'm guessing that Wells Fargo's collective correction has created an internal domino effect, one that has scrambled the bank's immune system for the better, infusing a strong dose of common sense *and* empathy back into the organization. In hindsight, the bank did what was necessary. They adjusted the organization in a gradual way until it achieved maximum success, and then announced that success to the world. In Wells Fargo's case, the bank placed oversized ads in newspapers, apologizing and promising to "fix what went wrong." The company issued a mandate that they would put customers' interests first and operate with full transparency. Employees heard this too. Only time will tell whether this new transparency will restore consumer trust, render company politics obsolete, and bring back regular deposits of common sense to the organization.

5

YOU HAVE BEEN DENIED ACCESS TO THIS CHAPTER

A COUPLE OF YEARS AGO, I BOUGHT a ticket for the Heathrow Express, an eighteen-minute-long train shuttle service that runs between London's Paddington Station and Heathrow Airport. As I stood there on the platform waiting for the train, I noticed a sign I hadn't seen before. OUR TEAM HAS THE RIGHT TO WORK FREE FROM VERBAL AND PHYSICAL ABUSE, the sign read. THESE WILL NOT BE TOLERATED UNDER ANY CIRCUMSTANCES. WE ARE COMMITTED TO FOLLOWING UP ON ALL REPORTS.

Signs like these are now being found all around the world. I get it. It's nice having an employer who looks out for you. But *physical* abuse? On the *Heathrow Express?* I could understand the occasional curse word now and then being lobbed at some cheeky young employee, but what could possibly put transportation employees at heightened risk of physical abuse?

When I asked around, the answer became clear. The Heathrow Express had replaced nearly a dozen human ticket agents with a small cluster of automated ticket machines. Every twenty minutes or so, roughly one hundred passengers had to wait in long lines to buy their tickets, with nearly everyone keeping a close eye on the overhead digital clock that was ticking down the minutes and seconds until the next train pulled in.

That wasn't even the worst part. When the machine finally produced their tickets, passengers then had to wait in another long line before eventually squeezing themselves through one of five narrow turnstiles. Anyone who was overweight, or disabled, or carrying a bulky suitcase had to be buzzed through a special gate, though from what I could tell, the gate agent seemed to have gone home for the day. Everyone was in a crazy rush, as well as frantic and annoyed, and telling anyone who would listen that they *had* to make the train, otherwise they would miss their flight and their connection and . . . I could see how some poor Heathrow Express worker might get a high heel thrown at his head.

It goes without saying that the Heathrow Express's zero-tolerance policy is a reflection of common sense — the good kind. No one would argue against it, especially now, in the wake of a pandemic, and no employee should spend his or her day getting yelled at by strangers or worse, clobbered by a shoe. But the reason *why* the Heathrow Express's zero-tolerance policy is good common sense is because of an underlying tech issue that makes *no sense whatsoever*.

It's like a physician giving you a medication, then writing a script for a second medication whose only purpose is to reduce the side effects of the first. Why not stop taking *both* medications, and save yourself time and trouble? In this case, why hadn't Heathrow Airport Holdings, the parent company of the Heathrow Express, thought through the consequences of installing an insultingly tiny number of ticket machines and turnstiles for thousands of daily passengers, many of them tourists and businesspeople lugging a week's worth of luggage behind them? Is it any wonder they became peevish when they were forced to line up behind machines and turnstiles as a mocking digital clock alerted them in real time that they were going to miss their train and flight? I don't know if this problem has now been resolved. Heathrow Express's zero-tolerance policy is laudable, and perhaps even necessary, but ... wasn't someone missing something in terms of its real-world application?

If you've ever taken a domestic flight anywhere in the United States, you've probably wondered if airlines are missing out on common sense too.

You get to the airport and take up position in yet another long check-in line. You shuffle along and twenty minutes later, you're at the head of the line. But where are all the ticket agents who are supposed to help you? Of the half-dozen booths across from you, only one is staffed by an actual human being, and a) he looks bored and distracted; b) he's not even looking in your direction; or c) he's on Twitter. Instead, a young airline attendant with a nametag gestures you toward what looks like a slot machine in a Reno restroom. Confused, your eyes flip back and forth between the slot machine and the vacant ticket booth. "Do I use the machine, or ... ?" you ask. "Machine," she says.

It's a digital world, after all. What a funny time to be alive.

The machine isn't a slot machine at all but an automated ticket kiosk. When you tap it, the screen comes to life, and asks for your passport or driver's license. Flattening out the former as best you can, you insert it inside a slot. *Your document cannot be read,* the machine says. Turning your passport over, you give it another shot. "I must be doing something wrong," you call out to the attendant, and somehow she gets the thing to work.

The machine now asks you to enter your reservation number. What *is* your reservation number? Where is that Travelocity email confirmation you remember printing out? A frantic pat-down search yields a sheet of soggy white paper inside the back pocket of your jeans. It's your confirmation email! You then key in the right numbers, so why does the machine reject them? You press TRY AGAIN, but you get the same result. "I'm so sorry," you call over to the attendant, who has her hands full helping another passenger. "I can't seem to get this thing to work." When she comes over, it turns out you entered your *Travelocity* number, not your *reservation* number! Unfortunately, the second number is also rejected by the machine. "That's weird," she murmurs.

Five minutes later she's managed to figure it out, and now she darts off to help other passengers who are cawing at her. But the machine isn't done with you yet. Are you checking bags, and if so, how many? You surrender your debit card and wait there as the machine processes the hard-to-believe $30 charge. The machine tells you to take your bag over to the counter.

Okay, *stop*. Stop right *here*. Why install automated ticketing kiosks in the first place if so many airline passengers either need help using them or end up at the ticket counter anyway to check their bags? Is this a modern-day version of *Candid Camera*? Who thought up this process? Nonetheless, you wheel your suitcase over to the counter. It takes some time to find the agent, but eventually he comes over and tags your bag. Thanking him, you start making your way in the direction of security, when he calls out, "Hold on!" Apparently, it's no longer his job to place your suitcase on the conveyor belt directly behind him. It's *your* job! It's some crazy new perk of being *you!* Along with paying the airlines $30 for a service that used to be on the house, you now get to lug your suitcase five hundred feet to what looks like a makeshift tent and . . . deposit it there, which you do. All the while wondering, *What's the point of all this technology if it all ends up like this?*

"The system was designed by someone who is not thinking," says Customer Experience Consultant Ian Golding. "It's a complete breakdown in how to leverage digital tech. Airports have made something so simple so ridiculously overcomplicated."

It's also a symptom of something bigger.

It's impossible to write about the negative effects of technology without sounding crabby, old, or willfully out-of-touch. *Why can't the culture go back to the way it once was? A time when kids played stickball on the street, teenagers listened to records, neighbors stopped to talk to one another, and the fly swatter was king?* These days, if you criticize tech in any way, you're seen as an old-school relic — a human gramophone. Basically, your opinions are irrelevant. No one is listening to you, and if they do it's with a little smirk. Technology is bigger than

> In one company, the lights all shut off automatically after ten minutes, when sensors determined rooms were empty. Unfortunately, that meant that soon after the start of any meeting, the room, and everyone in it, was plunged into blackness.

any one person, and nothing you can say will change *anything*.

So why do I risk sounding like a crusty old farmer by blaming technology as one of the biggest factors contributing to the death of common sense?

The answer is that the same digital innovations and accelerations that were designed to improve and streamline our lives have ended up in many cases complicating them. Needlessly, too. To the point where a lot of the time you and I are often on the edge of frustration and rage.

As my friend, Pinterest and Lyft Board Member Mark Thompson, notes, "Tech is a truculent force not likely to be regulated at the pace that it evolves in the market. Phones and pharmaceuticals, cars and construction, all make life better. More relevant is to place our efforts on how to make tech serve us, rather than us becoming its slave."

Today we volley between those two poles, with the various modern-day machines at Paddington Station and in U.S. airports plainly illustrating our anxiety. Look, I'm not saying that any company today can, or should, survive without tech, especially after COVID-19. That's just not going to happen. But the attempts on the part of some businesses to speed up and infuse technology into their procedures just for the sake of using technology defies common sense a lot of the time. The truth is, sometimes tech can ultimately turn what should be a straightforward, frictionless experience into a sustained roar of helplessness and fury from customers, which is only increased when they are forced to simply accept this as the way things are and will continue to be.

For example, two years ago, Swiss International Air Lines was doing its best to cut down on costs in its headquarters. It hired a vendor, who said he could save the company money *and* energy. A few months later, every office in Swiss International Air Lines headquarters was outfitted with a system that shuts off all the lights automatically after ten minutes, when sensors determine that a room has no one in it. What company wouldn't love to save on their electric bill and, by preserving energy, help save the planet? There was only one problem, a dark one: the new sensors often confused stillness and focus for absenteeism. Ten minutes into any meeting, the lights would abruptly shut off, plunging the room, and everyone in it, into blackness. It was actually somewhat terrifying. It felt like the world had ended, that the power grid had been compromised by hackers, or that some sort of interloper was waiting outside in the bushes.

Anyhow, once employees got used to this particular glitch, it became something of a ritual for them to grope around in the dark and either wave or clap their hands to restore the electricity. Everyone in the company laughed and laughed about it, but the thing is, *no one even questioned it.*

For example, whenever someone in a company brings up a tech malfunction or setback — *The Wi-Fi is slow; this PowerPoint deck didn't come through* — the topic will come up so often that an hour later, it's pretty much all anyone has talked about. Faced with a frozen screen or a slow-moving server, most employees throw up their hands and surrender. They become less confident they can bring about any change in their company or pivot around regulations. The amount of time companies waste on the very thing that's designed to improve cost efficiency—and which ends up killing around 10 percent of all productivity in organizations—is staggering.

A colleague and I recently spent a week writing down in a notebook every time someone brought up a tech issue in a single company. Twenty-four hours later, the number of issues was up to sixty-seven. By the end of the week, we were both frankly so bored we'd quit counting. It's the same outside the office: *I'm late for dinner because Google Maps sent me to Buffalo. I ordered the tortellini, but the app gave me ziti. I never got your text; are you positive you sent it?* Recently a colleague and I went out to dinner with the president of a large corporation. My colleague drove, and I was in charge of getting us there. There was a lot of traffic, and at one point, realizing we'd be a few minutes late, my colleague asked if I minded calling our dining companion and apologizing in advance for our tardiness. I did, or at least I thought I did. "Hey, Tim," I said. "The traffic is horrible on the highway—I mean seriously slow. Anyway, we'll be with you soon, hopefully in fifteen minutes."

When we pulled up in front of the restaurant, I noticed a small crowd of people on the sidewalk. Tim was among them, and he and everyone else looked worried and concerned. "Are you okay?" he asked of me. I didn't understand. "Uh, yeah," I said. "I'm sorry we're late, but as I said in my voicemail, traffic was horrible." Later I found out why everyone on the sidewalk looked so mortified. The message I'd left on Tim's voicemail had been converted to text. With my semi-heavy Danish accent now scrambled into perfect English, it read: *Hey, Tim, the tariffs are horrible in this hospital. I was almost slaugh-tered, but someone will be with you in fifteen minutes.*

On and on it goes until you're convinced that tech and common sense, which you once assumed would work together seamlessly, will invariably be at cross-purposes. Put another way, tech often makes *us* feel crazy — when a lot of the time the problem is tech itself.

Look — companies require the latest software and gizmos to remain competitive. Yet very few of them take the time to think it through. Many global companies, for example, believe that if their employees collaborate openly, exchanging hard-won victories and war stories, everyone wins. But instead of taking the time to say, *Tim, this is Judy — Judy, meet Tim,* they invest in a suite of collaborative software, usually at preposterous expense. Some businesses have up to *ten* different collaborative software systems! But a few years later, they pull the plug. *Collaborative software doesn't work,* they say. *Right* — because no one took the time, or used their common sense, to figure out why.

Well, I'll tell you why! Most businesses assume that once they install software and flip a switch, it's a done deal — just as companies realized enormous cost savings during the COVID-19 pandemic thanks to employees working from home, without taking into consideration how put-upon and disconnected many of those employees felt, or that the very concept of *culture* was now moot. No, the assumption was that employees would begin collaborating just like that. No training or rollout necessary — just *go!* Why buy an additional, costly implementation service if the collaborative software is as awesome as everybody says? A few months later, this software, lacking an implementation plan, any follow-up, or even an exercise or two to normalize it for employees, accumulates dust until the next workgroup decides that the answer to everyone's problems is to buy yet *another* suite of collaborative software. Honestly, does that really make sense?

A different kind of common senselessness assails me every time I open up my laptop.

Do you have a PC, and if so, do you use Windows? Then I have a few questions. Why whenever I create a PowerPoint presentation does the arrow on the screen end up pointing in the opposite direction from where I dragged it? Whose idea was it to change all the colors on my screen and clutter the entire top pane? Why did Windows ask me to "select my favorite picture" among the dozen on offer, and when I chose a photograph of birds — because I love birds — it gave me a cat, that assassin of birds, instead? Why are Microsoft passwords long, awkward, and hard to type? Why whenever I need help with a Windows-related issue does it take forty-five minutes to locate the Microsoft HELP button? Why is there both a SEARCH *and* a FIND button? Shouldn't *searching* lead to *finding,* or am I being childish? Why, when I see that Skype or Microsoft Office has an update, do I avert my eyes, knowing that if I press INSTALL, my laptop will shut down for what often feels like several decades, and that once it restarts in the year 2060, Skype won't let me back in unless I enter my Microsoft account number? (And since when have I had a Microsoft account number? Are Microsoft and Skype the same? I guess . . . now they are.) Why does Zoom cap their meetings at forty minutes? Does "forty" *mean* something?

Has your iPhone battery ever died? Apple once proclaimed that their batteries have 250 hours on standby mode, forgetting, maybe, that iPhones *don't work when they're in standby mode.* Also, why, when you create a new contact in your iPhone is there a Home category when no one you know owns a landline anymore?

It may sound like I'm picking on Microsoft and Apple, but similar issues apply to *all* computers. It's not just clutter, varying colors, or passwords that look like driveway gravel and decisions made in-house by bored IT guys with no consideration for customers that bother me. No, actually, the biggest issue I have with tech is that it erases our common sense by detaching us from our own empathy. While Skyping or Zooming with a friend, how often have you found yourself "just" checking Instagram or Twitter, "just" scanning the CNN headlines or "just" checking the weather forecast, now and again inserting "Uh-huh" and "Yeah" and "Totally!" like a series of randomly placed bookmarks, thereby wiping away empathy from the conversation?

Think about it. Along with common sense, our intuition has evolved over centuries and is an integral part of human DNA. We know to run for cover if a lion appears on our porch. We know to respond to a crying baby. But gradually, and with almost no resistance, we've permitted technology and data to overwrite centuries of accumulated human intuition—intuition deriving from the experience of unnumbered generations—some of whom I assume were, at least in the aggregate, *as* smart as we are.

Quick: tell me all the phone numbers you know by heart. Five? Three? Two? Your own? Tell me how to get to the hospital in the next town without using Google Maps. You have no idea where that hospital is, do you? Data tells us whether our local Thai restaurant is open or closed. It tells us how many stars a stranger gave to the pad Thai and whether that stranger subtracted a half star from the curry puffs because the waitress was, in her opinion, "kind of cold."

Will it be sunny or rainy today? Only the data on your laptop knows, though most of us have had the experience of seeing the raindrop icon on a bright afternoon when the windows are open, and everyone is running around in their bathing suits. In fact, whenever friends of mine plan a party or an event, they continuously check the upcoming weather report. If there's no sun, they'll check another forecast, and then another. Technology has somehow led them to believe that if they dig hard enough, they'll locate the perfect day, which they can then "save," guaranteeing everyone a good time.

Day by day, our brains are adapting to shortcuts, to easy, half-baked solutions, and to others doing the deciding *for* us. Stop to consider what would happen and how we would respond, or even cope, if someone took this crutch away from us!

The worldwide multiplication of data gives rise to a question: What does it mean anymore to "know" something? What does it mean to have an instinct, a vibe, or a gut feeling about something or someone? Is data *really* superior to our emotions, instincts, and intuition? No, but we sure act like it is. If data conflicts with our gut or if an answer can only be found online, we eventually lose faith in our own instincts, intuition, and sensitivity to know certain things without knowing why we know them. We begin looking at the world through *processes* or *systems* or both. And yes, three decades from now it's very possible that computers will be able to replicate or at least approximate intuition. But for right now they don't.

As smartphones, tablets, and laptops monopolize our work and personal lives, the opportunities to follow common sense — and empathy — don't present themselves as often as they used to. We feel compelled to squeeze every free moment we have into something productive, squashing any space or time for reflection. Once, eating breakfast or driving to the airport was a time for pensive rumination. Today breakfasts and car rides have both been converted into work time. Computers, tablets, and phones need to defragment their memories now and again. If we never power them down, our devices get slower and slower — and our brains are no different. As technology use multiplies, increasing our aloneness and self-sufficiency, empathy levels plummet. The same quality that made humans such a successful species is the thing we've chosen to abandon, and with it, of course, goes common sense.

Irascible as I know I may sound, technology is erasing common sense in company after company. Before the internet, bosses interviewed prospective employees face-to-face. Today those same interviews are often done on Skype or even on AI software, which conducts the whole interview with candidates, assessing their skills and abilities more on the basis of eye movement, word usage, and voice hesitations and less on their verbal responses. Even before COVID, a few of the largest banks in Australia, for example, have totally eliminated face-to-face meetings, relying instead on a shortlist of job candidates, all compiled by computers and only crossing desks for final approval.

Last time I looked, I didn't think that common sense was a technological breakthrough that AI had fully conquered. Nor could I have imagined that the worldwide excuse of "I'm busy," one shaped in no small part by technology, would serve as a very common reason many companies and employees use for *not* embracing common sense.

Ask any friend or acquaintance how they're doing these days or how they've been or what they've been up to, and I can guarantee you that their immediate response will be *Busy — you? Yeah, so busy*. Whether we're talking about our work or private lives, not one of us can resist the temptation to tell everyone we know just how *overwhelmed* we are.

Why? Because being busy, or at least saying we are, validates our existence. More than most words, "busy" is thick with implication. "Busy" implies that we're popular, needed, in demand, good at what we do, and even able to juggle multiple projects simultaneously. When was the last time you said you weren't doing anything, that you had too much time on your hands, or that you were taking the day off? Almost no one says that! If you did, your friends would either pretend they didn't hear you or change the subject. *Poor guy, no work, no friends, no life*.

In addition, technology enhances the perception that we're in a race against a ticking clock, and that if for some reason we can't outpace the present moment, we're likely to fall behind permanently and probably fatally. Have you ever been on Twitter, casually scrolling through Tweets, when a bubble suddenly appears: SEE NEW TWEETS! Something in your chest drops. You opened Twitter only thirty seconds ago, and you're already living in the past. The present moment has somehow lapped you. Tech feeds time amphetamines. Every minute we have needs to be optimized — spent learning, scanning, keeping tabs on our upcoming tasks, staying vigilant about the worst things that can happen.

I might be fully imagining it and it might be anecdotal, but today we speak using shorter sentences. We walk faster than we did ten years ago. Whenever I'm driving on the highway, it seems that more and more cars travel in the passing lane, with the regular lane reserved exclusively for slowpokes, stoners, and texters as well as elderly drivers (who probably have no fluency in tech). Under technology, the human brain reminds me of nothing so much as one of those illuminated overhead screens in airports and train stations, where times, destinations, and gate numbers are in a constant state of flicking and churning, vanishing suddenly, popping up over there, reappearing on the top row, dropping to the second or third row, flicking and churning again, and finally, like a love interest who meets your glance in a significant way, the screen tells you your flight is boarding at Gate 37.

With time the priority in most business—versus long-range thinking—is it any wonder that common sense is so lacking in companies? Common sense requires a sense of real pause. And real perspective. It requires that we understand and acknowledge other people's points of view. But seriously, who has time for that these days?

Along with validating our existence, busyness also creates a sense of *belonging*. Listen in on any conversation before or after a Zoom meeting, and you'll hear the same verses of the same dull song: *How are you, Jim? Busy. Surviving, though. How about you, Tom? Hanging in there—crazy busy, actually. Okay, Jim, have a good one, don't kill yourself. You too, Tom, don't work too hard.* Technology has come up with a bunch of new signals that attest to our industry: the amount of emails in our inbox; the number of appointments in our online calendars; how often we're cc'd on other people's correspondence.

One of the many problems with busyness is that cluttering our brains actually makes us *less* productive. The global trend of everybody being as busy as they are means that the more we justify that fact, the less time we have for ourselves, to come up with new and imaginative ideas or to just sit back, reflecting. Certainly, we have no time to think about our jobs, where our company is heading, or in what departments common sense might be totally lacking and what we can do to fix them.

I once read about an informal experiment carried out by a Canadian marketing expert named Paul Ralph. Observing that everyone in his immediate circle was telling him about how "busy" they were, Ralph and his wife decided that for the next year, they wouldn't use that word. How would *not* saying they were busy affect their behavior, or even their lives?

The changes were immediate. Ralph and his wife began engaging with their friends more deeply and authentically. They didn't realize how bad they'd been making others feel. They felt happier, freer, more in control of the choices they made. "More importantly," Ralph writes, "when *we* quit using the word 'busy,' we noticed that others did the same . . . Busy, it would seem, is a self-fulfilling prophecy. The more we said it, the more we felt it. The more we felt it, the more we acted like it."

If technology is responsible for helping to erode common sense, gnawing away at our collective human empathy and creating a class of busyness that Robert Louis Stevenson described more than two hundred years ago as "a symptom of deficient vitality," companies also use technology as an excuse for loopy, maddening behavior. Here's a classic example of when common sense was seemingly not included:

Last year, I gave two speeches at one of the largest food and beverage companies in the world. The organization is quite profitable and is a household name, but for the purposes of this story, let's just call it FoodaCo. I did some consulting work there, billed them, and awaited the payment. Famous last words. But maybe it's better to start from the beginning.

On February 22, 2019, my company's CFO, Allan, sent out the first of three invoices to FoodaCo. Three weeks went by. On March 19, the FoodaCo team contacted me to discuss a future event in which I could maybe play a role, and a week later, on March 25, it confirmed the event. *Awesome,* I thought. This was promising. After all, if you were hiring someone to give a keynote speech, wouldn't you want to stay on that person's good side by paying him what you owed him pretty promptly? It would *seem* that way. Unfortunately, the invoice sent to FoodaCo on February 22 was now more than a month late, so Allan issued a polite reminder.

Something seemed to click, because a day later, the FoodaCo team emailed Allan, asking him to reconfirm that the invoice he had sent was payable in U.S. dollars, even though the invoice stated clearly in bold letters that the amount due should be paid in U.S. currency. Allan confirmed the obvious. Sometime in the course of this back-and-forth, FoodaCo mentioned that it was in the process of setting up my company as a vendor in its system. That probably explained the holdup in payment.

On April 5, almost two and a half months after that first invoice was sent out, the FoodaCo team engaged in additional discussions about the future event it wanted me to be a part of. Allan sent out the second of the three invoices. A week later, he issued a reminder to the FoodaCo team: the first invoice was now more than a month late; would the company please pay it as soon as possible? On April 24, Allan sent out yet another reminder. The first invoice still hadn't been paid — it was now three months late — and the second invoice was six days overdue.

The FoodaCo team responded, though not with payment. Surely by now, it said, we'd received an email with instructions about how to sign up for the company's third-party payment system? Well, I'd gotten offers for Cialis, bed bug exterminators, fungus removing spices, wrinkle erasers, CBD lotions, and a special Russian lady who wants to be my friend, but no email about any third-party payment system had appeared in my company inbox. The FoodaCo team forwarded a link to the sign-up page of the third-party vendor, a global electronic invoicing firm known as Tungsten Network.

Unfortunately, the Tungsten Network's sign-up link didn't work. When Allan contacted the Tungsten support team, it told him no, the link sent by the FoodaCo team didn't work. Perhaps discerning an edge in Allan's voice, it helped him sign up for the system another way. We were getting closer.

Well, kind of, sort of. Before the Tungsten system could confirm our identity, we needed to "request a connection with the customer" — that is, FoodaCo — to alert the company that we had requested this connection. If we didn't, we wouldn't be able to submit any invoices via the third-party payment system. Allan emailed the FoodaCo team, asking it to approve the connection. Numerous emails passed back and forth. This was starting to get a little nutty. We just wanted to get paid! Instead, nothing was happening, and nothing was happening incredibly slowly too.

Contacting FoodaCo once again, Allan asked the team politely and then more insistently, to approve the connection created by the third-party payment system. FoodaCo's response, when it came, was almost childlike. The team wasn't sure how the Tungsten Network system worked, and there wasn't much it could do on its end. Sure, there was! It could approve the damn connection and get us paid! A day later, FoodaCo came back to us. Someone at the company had discussed this issue with another department, and it seemed *we* were the ones responsible for making the connection. The problem, or so they claimed, was all on our end. It was *our* fault!

Except that wasn't true.

Allan circled back to the Tungsten Network support team. Had their members *really* been in touch with the FoodaCo team? Could they confirm that FoodaCo was responsible for confirming the connection? Yes, they could! It *wasn't* our fault after all! Armed now with the details that Tungsten Network had used to contact FoodaCo in the first place, Allan forwarded the information on to the FoodaCo team. And waited.

Great news! FoodaCo *approved the connection!* It also set up a new vendor code for our company. Both invoices – the one from February 22, and its brother, from April 5 – were submitted via the system and officially received by FoodaCo. Confirmation! Action! The wheels of the train were turning!

Then, abruptly, they stalled. The train ground its way back to the train shed. Another week went by. It was now May 6.

Allan sent an email to the FoodaCo team, really, truly *urging* the company to pay the two outstanding invoices. *We* had people *we* needed to pay.

The FoodaCo team floated a few excuses. Nothing as fatuous as *The alarm clock didn't go off* or *The puppy ate my algebra homework,* but nothing terribly credible either. A day later, Allan sent the third of our three invoices to the FoodaCo team.

Receiving no response, he sent yet another follow-up reminder to FoodaCo. FoodaCo came back with a bunch of new excuses.

On May 15, a call came in from another FoodaCo employee from another department. Even though Allan had sent the banking details for wiring numerous times, the person on the other end said she needed to verify our banking details, the wiring codes and so on. Never mind that Allan had done all this before, over and over again too. The point seemed to be that something — anything — was happening, and this was cause for celebration. Allan verified the details. Momentum! Action!

When a few days passed without any payments showing up, Allan sent them another email reminder. An hour later, the phone rang. It was — you guessed it — FoodaCo. Another employee from yet another department needed to cross-check our banking details, not just with our CFO but with another member of our team. Apparently, it was longstanding FoodaCo policy to verify banking details with two independent employees (even though FoodaCo had wired a payment to our company only five months earlier). This seemed like just one more runaround.

Twenty-four hours later, when the payment still hadn't

shown up, Allan placed yet another call to the FoodaCo team. He was met with an additional round of excuses.

By now, four months had gone by since we sent the first invoice to FoodaCo. On May 21, our lawyer contacted FoodaCo and brought up the possibility of legal action if the outstanding invoices weren't paid at once. Later that day, the company confirmed it was sending out a check. A check? What about those wiring instructions that the company had requested, and Allan had provided 750 times? A check would take *days* to arrive, and a week or so to clear! Two hours later, my bank confirmed that payment for the first two invoices had come in. The next morning, the payment for the remaining invoice showed up. Oh, one more thing: thirty days later, a check arrived in the mail. It still hangs on our office wall. So at least they were telling the truth about *that*.

Larger companies especially have become adept at delaying payments, using all sorts of devious tricks and excuses, and routinely blaming technology, to avoid paying their bills on time while collecting the interest on *their* end. For companies like FoodaCo, I gather it's just common sense ... but for the rest of us, who have our own bills to pay, it's beyond ridiculous.

So what would happen if we *didn't* have technology? If we stepped outside it for a few days? How would it affect us? Would things get worse, better, or both, and in what ways?

Ask Maersk. In the summer of 2017, the company became the victim of a major cyberattack.

On June 27, without warning, every one of Maersk's computer screens worldwide went black. To avoid further

Today we speak using shorter sentences. We walk faster than we did ten years ago. So what would happen if we *didn't* have technology? For Maersk, the answer arrived involuntarily when the company became the victim of a major cyberattack.

infection, the company shut down all its remaining systems, suspending contact with one-fifth of every active ship on earth. Most employees, not knowing what to do, simply went home. Maersk CEO Søren Skou issued a statement, asking all his employees in 121 countries to "do what you think is right to serve the customer – don't wait for the HQ, we'll accept the cost."

Technology and complex databases have always been at the heart of Maersk's business. When the company's computer servers suddenly stopped working, no one had any idea what to do. For the first time, the company fully realized its impact on the world – that as a result of a targeted cyberattack, one in five ships in the world was now standing absolutely still in the water. In the face of a catastrophe, what was "right for the customers and the business"? Unfortunately, the answer couldn't be found online.

As painful as the cyberattack was, something strange, unanticipated, and positive came out of it. Ulf Hahnemann, Maersk's global human resources officer, later told me, "The hierarchy was momentarily suspended, and the organization immediately increased engagement, and moved faster, with a feeling of freedom, where employees felt trusted to do what *they* believed was right." Why? Because the only option left for Maersk employees was to *visit their clients*. In person. Door-to-door. Face-to-face.

Louisa Loran, Maersk's global head of business development and marketing recalls, "It was Maersk at its best. It didn't matter what your title was. The mindset was, 'If I have to stand in a terminal gate, and tell a trucker to stop at Slot 18, well, I'll do whatever is necessary.'"

Overnight, and at great financial cost, a company hampered by complex processes, compliance laws, and legal restrictions was set free. That's not to say it was easy. Having digitized everything that could be digitized to cut costs, Maersk employees were used to seeing their clients as mere numbers. It was a keyboard relationship — transactional, efficient, and rational. Never mind that Maersk employees were human, and their clients were too.

At first clients were confused. Sorry, but *who* are these people who say they work for Maersk? Maersk employees were just as unused to dealing face-to-face with their customers. For both, the experience was transformative. Older employees, who dimly recalled a pretechnological time, adjusted to it faster than younger ones, who'd never known anything other than computer screens and keyboards. With those screens dark, they realized that different people in the company could end up making the biggest difference.

Inside Maersk, a group of employees mobilized a WhatsApp phone chain. Everyone was tasked to contact one person they knew in another country — and ask that person to do the same thing. Using her iPad and an external server, Louisa issued official Maersk communications to 2.1 million recipients every three hours for several days in a row.

This return to a basic common-sense response and sense

of empathy benefited *everyone,* especially the company's customers. Many of them experienced a profound shift in their mindsets. There was a collective adjustment. They could suddenly empathize with *Maersk's* pain. Company-client relationships had never felt more genuine. A new cohesion and an improved spirit came over the company. With bosses now walking the floors twice a day, employees felt a sense of real purpose, some for the first time. Many of them told me that Maersk's old entrepreneurial spirit had returned. Yes, the cyberattack was catastrophic for some of their clients and for the bottom line, but when the computers were up and running again, there were only upsides. Maersk and its clients actually began working together *better.*

What took place in the wake of the cyberattack brought into sharp focus the commonsensical principles I was trying to infuse in the company. As well as acknowledging the humanity of its own customers, Maersk was reminded that its customers had customers too. If Ford was late in receiving a shipment of cars, dealers and customers also suffered. If Home Depot's delivery got rolled, stores all across the United States would be out of stock.

The truth is, this isn't an issue that technology can address. Tech can create stunningly comprehensive lists on a screen. It can reveal names, dates, facts, figures, estimates, and projections. The right algorithms can be spectacular in their ability to free-associate, to predict how past habits create future behaviors. Then tech hits a wall. Lacking creativity and imagination, it can't go any deeper than that. Here is where human beings need to step in.

Our collective love affair with technology should be seen strictly as developmental and thus incomplete. But we're still in a state of asphyxiation and imbalance. It's the same with any discovery – sex, alcohol, cigarettes, exercise, a new favorite food. We go overboard. We can't get enough. We don't know what *enough* is. We romance strangers, drink or smoke or eat too much. Over time, we pull back. We negotiate with ourselves. We weigh pluses and minuses. We find some in-between place, and we try to maintain it.

Right now, we're still in the discovery period of learning what tech can and can't do, what it gives and clears away, what it can replace, and what, on the other hand, is irreplaceable, mysterious, and, you might even say, timeless. On that list is humanity, which in turn encompasses empathy and, of course, common sense. This same common sense will, I hope, someday free us from our servitude and help us recognize that in the end we – and not tech – are still the ones in charge.

6

SHOW ME YOUR DECK!

Have you ever gotten scalded by an overflowing cup of hot coffee? I certainly hope not. Still, one large company took its "less is more" philosophy to an extreme in the employee kitchen, which actually ended up *wasting* money. Here's how: in an attempt to save on coffee costs, the COO reduced the amount of coffee that trickled into employees' cups whenever they pushed the coffee machine button.

Most employees responded to this shortfall by pressing the button twice, producing so much coffee it overflowed over the tops of their mugs. No one wanted to risk carrying a hot full mug of coffee back to their desks, so most employees poured an inch or so of coffee out into the sink before returning to their desks.

How about a cup of common sense if we're trying to cut back on costs?

MEETINGS — AND POWERPOINT PRESENTATIONS — can eat up close to 50 percent of our time when we work in a company. It's a percentage few people are eager to acknowledge, perhaps because it's a reminder of just how poorly organizations (and the people who work in them) administrate their own time. The average company has meetings that center around plans, future plans, and lack of plans, meetings that analyze where previous plans went wrong and how to make future plans work better. There are meetings about strategies and the company's inability to strategize. Every last thing demands a meeting, even if no one has anything of value to say or conclude. In fact, having nothing to say or conclude is a capital reason to schedule a meeting, so why don't I send you an Outlook invite now!

With the end objective of restoring common sense to companies, their employees, and, of course, the consumers who buy and use what those companies sell, let's rewind to what happened a few weeks ago during the Wednesday morning Zoom staff meeting.

The meeting's about to start! Who's going to be there? Paula, Ogden, Niall, and Yolanda. Also, Jamie, Celeste, Tony, Louisa, Andres, and Bob A and Bob B (to tell them apart).

It's your seventh meeting so far this week, and you're only halfway to the weekend. The meetings in this company are . . . freaking endless. This company has meetings the way some houses have ants. If this organization had its way, you would be in back-to-back meetings all day and into the late evening.

This week alone included the status meeting, the project

group meeting, the review meeting, the approval meeting, the quarterly meeting, and two other meetings you can't remember. Your presence was required at each one. Well, "required" isn't the right word. Your *boss* was online. You *had* to show up, if only to show her just how hard you work, how on top of things you are, and to remind her of your unmatched verbal, organizational, and technological command. This week's litany of meetings now blurs with an equally time-squandering number of conference calls summarizing reports and requesting decks and status updates, culminating in even more meetings being scheduled—review meetings, committee meetings—and so on.

By this point, you feel you can read your colleagues' minds. Everyone is eager to say something clever or incisive to elevate their status. Instead, most of the time they come out with jewels (okay, in truth they're closer to old gum wrappers) like "I agree with Marco" or "I'm totally onboard, Roberta." If someone dislikes a concept, they'll say, "Great idea, I love it, but can we park that for a second? Jamie, any additional thoughts . . . ?"

It's funny, when you think about it, how people in meetings say the same things over and over again. Such as,

Can you hear me?
Can you see me?
(Weird breathing)
Oops, sorry, you go ahead.
Sorry, no, you first.
Oops, sorry, you go, no . . .
I was just going to say that . . .

How does everyone feel about . . . ?

(Weird crunching sound)

Sorry, guys, that was just Oscar, my dog.

My cat is sick — I'm so sorry.

Hey — sorry, guys, but I have to hop on another Zoom . . .

Many meetings, as you know, consist of a clump of middle managers sitting around second-guessing how Mike, the CEO, would respond. *Mike wouldn't agree with that* is a typical comment, as well as *I know Mike, and I can tell you right now that Mike is allergic to that stuff.* Everyone is competing to prove they know Mike better than the next person (for his part, Mike barely knows any of their names). Personally speaking, the few times you've proposed something out-of-the-ordinary to Mike, he's always said, "I love it!" Proving either that people are as multifaceted as red diamonds or, more likely, that nobody knows anything.

It's that time again.

You remove your pajamas and put on the Zoom shirt that hangs from your desk chair, praying no one notices it's the 127th day in a row you've worn it, and log on. Your face appears, amid eleven other faces. No one seems to know where to aim their eyes. The green laptop light? Two inches below that? Jamie and Celeste are too close to the screen, like calves nuzzling, and others sit at a prim distance, straight-backed, like kids in detention. Andres has his tablet angled in such a way that only one ear and a glasses temple are visible, and Louisa hasn't even turned her video on. But no one wants to bring that up, since Louisa probably just stumbled out of bed. Gone are the days when people awoke at 7 a.m. in anticipation of a 9 a.m. meeting. Now they wake up at 8:50 a.m., slam down a cup of coffee, and switch on their laptops, that is, if they ever turned them off.

Where in the world is Paula Zooming from? A slaughter-house? Are those ribs hanging from a hook, or a dark coat? Tony has the now-familiar Golden Gate Bridge as his back-drop. You can't help but wonder what he's hiding. You are frankly tired of seeing the Golden Gate Bridge—or any other emblems of space, freedom, and the prospect of someday leaving your house—during Zoom meetings. Still, it's better than the woman you read about who, unable to adjust her fil-ter, showed up for an online staff meeting as a potato.

As you and your colleagues wait for Yolanda, and Andy from marketing, to arrive, you engage in the by-now de ri-gueur ten minutes of small talk. Once it was the weather, then it was the pandemic, and today it's all the various nuisances involved in working from home. "Oh—you know—hanging in there," most people say when asked how they are. "It is what it is, right?" someone says. "It is what it is," you repeat. Se-riously, were you *always* this listless, or has working mostly from home just gotten you down?

The people who actually make the decisions in this com-pany generally show up five to ten minutes late, which ex-plains why Yolanda and Andy haven't made an appearance. Yes, they're both busy, important, and in demand, but they're also making a show of their superior status. "I just sent Yolanda an invite," Roberta says. "I did, too," several others chime in, which means that Yolanda will be jabbing at a half-dozen Zoom links, five of which won't work. Yolanda's face appears finally, her mouth opening and closing before some-one says, "Yolanda, you're on mute," a comment that crisscrosses with "For some reason we can't hear you, Yolanda, is your MUTE button on?" Yolanda unmutes herself and says, "Don't anyone dare ask me to repeat that!" Everyone laughs, though it's not funny.

No sign yet of Andy. "Why don't we give him five more minutes?" you propose, distracted as always by the various ping and dong sounds coming from people's online calendars. Paula adds that just now she sent Andy an email reminding him of the 9 a.m. start, inquiring if there's a time that works better for him. *Snap, Paula, who knew you were so passive-aggressive?* When there's still no Andy after five minutes, the meeting moves ahead without him. Someone can catch him up afterward; they always do.

You launch into a well-rehearsed explanation of this quarter's earnings bump, when you suddenly hear a jumble of random beeps and buzzing noises. "I'm Andy from marketing . . . Wait, is this thing even working?" "Andy—try changing your output settings," someone says (whatever those are.) "Maybe your mike is picking up the echo from your speakers," someone else tosses out.

With Andy aboard, it's time for the PowerPoint. Whenever a PowerPoint presentation is on the docket, everyone's attention begins to drift. You could swear you can hear multiple tabs opening, the zing of outgoing text messages, a screen door opening and closing, and the unmistakable sound of someone peeing. Ogden and Celeste both appear to be on a second Zoom meeting, and Celeste has forgotten to mute herself. "Totally, Pierre," you hear her say. "You'll have it by the end of the day." *Who's Pierre?* "If everyone could turn on their MUTE button, that would be great," says Paula. *Dammit, Paula, you're on fire!*

By now you've lost count of the number of times you've heard colleagues brag that they're running two conference calls at the same time. Productivity is evidently measured by how many online meetings you have back-to-back, without a rest, a bathroom break, a shower, eating, standing, getting exercise, or changing your clothes. It's as if the more meeting invitations people accept, the more points they'll get. Others just want to show everyone else how busy they are. As a result, no one has time to prepare for anything — especially meetings. How could they? This in turn leads to a huge increase in side meetings. Meetings begetting side meetings that beget more meetings, and on and on it goes.

In my experience, pretty much all businesspeople love to say how much they hate meetings. They believe they're a colossal waste of time, in part because despite the shiny eyes of the participants, the scrawling of notes on tablets and in margins, and the steady, affirmative rocking-chair motion of male and female heads, the collective attention span in most meeting rooms is, to put it nicely, limited. Everyone in attendance is preparing, at least in their heads, for their next meeting, and the one after that.

How is this common sense?

As I said earlier, common sense and empathy are irreversibly aligned. Empathy brings people together, allowing them to experience what it feels like to walk in someone else's shoes. If scheduling one meeting after the next exists only for the purpose of scheduling meetings, those meetings become nothing more than echo chambers that play back a company's internal beliefs and biases. Organizations are, quite simply, feeding the monster. Worse, rarely is anything accomplished, further wasting everybody's time.

Also, if one of the genuine benefits of a meeting is bringing together cross-functional teams, why are so few meetings cross-functional? Marketing typically has one meeting, while operations has another. The marketing department may come up with a solid plan or strategy, only to be overruled by operations, which votes it down for safety reasons during its own meeting. Why didn't marketing and operations come together and share a meeting room in the first place?

Let's jump back in:

This particular online meeting isn't as awful as some. Like the one five days ago.

There must have been a hundred people on that Microsoft Teams meeting. It was like a rave. Imagine attending an in-person meeting with a hundred other people. You'd lose your mind. Isn't there a digital fire code that restricts the number of participants in one online event? Why isn't there one?

A big reason for that Microsoft Teams meeting was so that Pete could present his PowerPoint. "Can everyone see my screen?" he kept asking. *No. No, Pete, no one can see your screen! Stop asking "Can everyone see my screen?" and do something!*

You've always associated Pete with acronyms. Five minutes into the meeting, he had already name-dropped the QCR, the UTS and the MMS. The two new employees nodded and scribbled notes, or at least showed scribbling body language. Maybe acronyms, like COVID, are contagious, because Sophie asked, "Pete, did your team take into account the increased pressure, which is only going to get worse in my opinion, from the QTPs?"

"We're on that," Pete said, "and even better, it's NKO-compliant. Did everyone get my deck?" Ninety-eight heads nodded, and two faces froze as their owners desperately flipped through their inboxes to find the deck in an unopened email. Two people asked if Pete would resend the deck, and two others chimed in with "I never got it" and "I don't think I was on the distribution list."

As Pete began his presentation, everyone in the room settled in for a tedious ride. One of your colleagues yawned with his mouth closed — a trick he once told you he mastered in business school and has refined over the years. Everything went as expected until the moment Larry appeared online. Larry is Pete's boss. His appearance seemed to unnerve Pete, who began winding his way backward to his first few Power-Point slides, weaving in the feedback he'd received from others in the room to ensure that Larry appreciated the multitude of angles Pete stole from his colleagues and now claimed as his own. At least everyone now knew that that Pete was a virtual asshole.

He was also a petrified virtual asshole. "Pete, you're frozen," someone said, and it was true: Pete's motionless face was a snapshot of torment, like a Gustave Doré illustration from Dante's *Inferno*. When he came back to life he asked, "So what does everybody think?" A few seconds passed. "Can you repeat that, please?" someone finally asked. "You were frozen."

It's hardly the only online glitch you've experienced during an online meeting. It's not as bad as the colleague who turned on her screen share, giving everyone a close-up of a desktop folder entitled DIVORCE. Then there was the time Sheri was interrupted by a little boy asking "Where is my penis?" "Sorry, everyone," Sheri said, but when she turned to her son, her knee banged up against her desk, sending her laptop flying and shattering a lamp. Of course there was also Becky's boyfriend whose figure you once detected slithering across the floor so as to avoid the beam of her laptop camera.

A meeting should last no longer than *thirty minutes*. One way I ensure this in physical meetings is by bringing in a clock and telling everyone that the clock represents the accumulated salaries of everyone in the room.

A few minutes later, the meeting came to an end, though nine points remained on the agenda. The fact of the matter is, someone will have to schedule another meeting. Meanwhile, your colleagues were saying goodbye and waving like the Trapp Family Singers — since when does anybody wave when they leave a meeting? The funniest part is they'll all see one another in five minutes at the next meeting, this one on WebEx, or is it Google Hangouts? You'd hoped for an elegant farewell — as if romantic music were swelling and movie credits were scrolling — but instead you see the LEAVE MEETING icon. Reluctantly you press it. Are you sure you want to leave this meeting? the box asks. *No, of course not!* you feel like shouting. *You saw through me, you bastard! I want to die here!* "We got a lot accomplished, and I look forward to the next time," someone was saying, but the room was empty, an abandoned dance floor.

You'll see everybody fourteen more times this week, no, wait, fifteen, thanks to the Friday night Zoom cocktail hour (your boss, worried company culture was taking a hit during the pandemic, sent everyone an invite, with kids and pets welcome). You would rather get drunk alone with your cat, but it's not like you have a choice anymore. The thing about doing everything from home is that none of your usual excuses will work.

Does any of this seem familiar? Is it uncomfortably close to your own experiences in online and in-person meetings? If so, why do you no longer question it but instead go with the flow, trudging blindly forward, allowing common sense to dissipate slowly and finally disappear? Here are a few rules to running successful, *commonsensical* meetings:

No phones, no web-surfing, no emails, no texts. I once spoke at Google's headquarters in Mountain View, California. There were two hundred people or so in the audience. During my thirty-minute speech, I made eye contact with literally four people. Everyone else was on their laptops or phones. Sure, some employees were recording my speech, making virtual eye contact through the video camera function of their phones or tablets, but the effect was the same: *We have better things to do than listen to you.*

Consider investing in a basket or other receptacle. Meeting participants can place a sticky note on their phones, drop them in, and retrieve them when the meeting is over. (Frankly? If someone or something is *that* important, meet with that individual in person, and talk things through. If it's not urgent, it can wait.)

Establish an agenda. Regardless of whether your meeting is virtual or not, you need to ask yourself: What do I want to achieve in this meeting? Now go even further. If this is the first meeting of the day, ask everyone present to list their agendas, i.e., the one thing they want to achieve. When the session ends, the team leader might consider sending a short note to all the attendees, reiterating key decisions and directions, as a subtle reminder (and nudge) for everyone to stay focused.

In short, hammer down what this meeting is about. Never say you're there to "review" things. That's too broad a subject. Are you seeking approval or clarification? Then say so. Be as concrete as possible.

Keep to a time limit. Most meetings last an hour with, as we've just seen, five to seven minutes subtracted for trivial technical issues that need to be resolved. In fact, corporate life has somehow adopted an unspoken rule that meetings have to run sixty minutes, and if they don't, well, something's wrong. A meeting should last no longer than *thirty minutes*.

One way I ensure this in physical meetings is by bringing in a clock. I tell everyone that the clock represents the accumulated salaries of everyone in the room. I posit a guess that the lowest salary is probably $120 an hour, with the highest around $1,000. "We're all here together right now," I say. "Before even *starting* this meeting, this meeting already costs about $15,000. And having *me* here makes it *more* expensive. So let's start the clock." Fifteen or twenty minutes later, I point out that we've already wasted $4,000 on fiddling with IT problems — and we go forward from there. The physical presence of a clock helps participants pay attention to what they're actually doing or, rather, *supposed* to be doing. Unfortunately, I often have to truck the same clock over to the next meeting and to the one after that.

What does the clock do, exactly? Aside from being a running chronicle of time going by, everyone becomes mindful that a thirty-minute meeting needs to be productive. If they succeed in addressing everything on the agenda after twenty minutes, they don't *have* to use up the remaining ten minutes. Obviously, the clock is also great for basic timekeeping. If you used the meeting time productively, or wastefully, you will know it. The presence of a clock also makes a dent in small talk. By mapping how they spend their time, employees are often surprised that the common refrain of "There aren't enough hours in the day" comes as a result of too much web-surfing, too many coffee breaks, too much chitchat, and so on.

I'm a big believer in one of Elon Musk's productivity rules: "Walk out of a meeting, or drop off a call, as soon as it is obvious you aren't adding value. It is not rude to leave, it is rude to make someone stay and waste their time." In short, participants should feel free to leave a meeting if they feel they have nothing to contribute.

Be aware of "loop" thinking. The dialogue in meetings sometimes reminds me of a Ferris wheel. A conversation begins somewhere, rises, peaks, then returns, fretfully, to where it started, this time with dibs and dabs of resistance. Let's revisit how the conversation around the headphones I bought at the airport might go. "We've discussed the idea of making the headphones easier to remove from the cardboard," someone says. "But if we do that, what about theft?" "I want legal to take a long, hard look at safety issues. What if a child got hold of the cord and accidentally swallowed it?" "If we changed packaging, our production costs would go up." "My worry is that new packaging wouldn't fit on retailers' shelves." "But no one can get the headphones out of the plastic!" People offer criticism because it shows everyone else that they have good, analytical minds and are thinking things through. Things disintegrate, time is wasted, and nothing gets accomplished.

To avoid this common scenario, consider dividing up conversations in meetings into three phases. Imagine if in this same meeting, someone proposed the idea of creating a "mini-backpack" for the headphones, with space for your phone in the front pocket and a pocket on the side for an attached cord.

First, *if there were no technical or operational issues, do we like the idea in principle?* If everyone in the room supports the mini-backpack idea, then everyone can approve the essence or core of the decision that needs to be made.

Second, *what sort of pushback are we likely to receive?* Instead of running an open, ongoing dialogue among a dozen participants competing for the best, most powerful pushback, divide the room into groups of three. Convert the meeting, and the issue, into an unofficial workshop. Ask each group to identify one key issue and — most important of all — couple it with a *solution.*

Finally, *assemble everyone's issues and ideas on Post-it notes, then divide these up by color.* For example, the key issues go on a yellow Post-it note, and the solutions on a green one. Keep to one issue per note. Why? Because one reason that most meetings run longer than they should is that participants address the same topic over and over again. By using Post-it notes, you can park the issue, and the note, on the board under the category Already Addressed (which sends a clear signal that the issue is no longer up for debate). Also in this category is any idea that wasn't received well in the moment. That idea is now dead.

Everything doesn't have to be a meeting. What meetings do you remember, and why? Most people don't remember more than three things from any given meeting (at best). Consider all the communication tools organizations have at their disposal—emails, conference calls, reports, spreadsheets, PowerPoints, and so on. *Not everything merits a meeting.* In some ways, the fragmentation among company departments results in meetings playing a role they were never designed to play. Many people schedule and attend meetings because they're afraid of being forgotten or overlooked. Meetings thus become a validation that what you do matters. (More employees in large organizations than I can remember have expressed to me their fear that someday they'll be forgotten.)

The next time someone says, "Let's schedule a meeting next week," why not ask, "Wait—what *are* we meeting for?" If the goal of the proposed meeting is to reach agreement about some issue, maybe you don't need a meeting. Why not hammer out a yes or no answer then and there? If the conclusion is maybe and it's a cross-functional matter, with all functions attending, then yes, by all means go ahead and have the meeting.

If meetings are inimical to common sense a lot of the time, should they be eliminated? No—but I will say that their indiscriminate use has gotten completely out of proportion. The purpose is gone, replaced by habit and a passive and widespread acceptance that this is just how things are in the business world. But if you follow your common sense, it doesn't have to be that way.

It probably follows that the best meetings I've ever attended had one thing in common, namely, *no PowerPoint decks*.

Acknowledge up front the inherent limitations of online meetings. Needless to say, since the pandemic, online meetings have largely overtaken in-person meetings and become a staple in our lives. Most of us feel obliged to show up, too, as evidence of how "busy" we are.

Yet, in real life, how often are we asked to stand three feet away from our colleagues while staring at their faces for an hour? Everyone who has participated in a Zoom or Microsoft Teams meeting knows it's an unnatural medium. Time delays, echoes, distracting background sounds, frozen screens, and ongoing self-appraisals — *do I still look good on the camera?* — only complicate things. The inability to pick up on other people's body language further erodes our collective empathy. Silence online typically elicits anxiety. (Zoom and Teams should consider featuring an I'M THINKING button, which attendees could press to signal that they are ruminating.) Some employees suffer from Zoom fatigue, a consequence of spending most of the day with their eyes trained on their laptops or tablets. With the transition to online-only meetings, productivity may actually be falling. "Home" and "work" were already uncomfortably intertwined for most of us. But today, our companies and our colleagues have literally invaded our inner sanctums.

Siri, where's the CULTURE button in Microsoft Teams? The biggest victim of our new online environment is . . . culture. Seemingly inconsequential in-person encounters we have at work — two colleagues connecting in the hallway or in a side office or in the elevator — serve as invaluable synchronizations. Generally speaking, consensus building happens in smaller groups, in confined spaces, where we can safely express our thoughts. But when we're online, all that goes away. The conversation between two colleagues is now on display — but did they really want to share their opinions with nine other people?

For this reason, I begin any morning session with a five-minute breakout. I invite the team to gather in groups of three in a virtual breakout room. What are everybody's key challenges from the day before? (Showing vulnerability has a remarkable impact on others — it makes people human.) This five-minute breakout is a powerful way to get people to reconnect and synchronize before the "real meeting" gets underway.

Consider asking your colleagues to raise their hands if they have something to say. I'm surprised more online meeting attendees haven't thought of this. Zoom and Microsoft Teams meetings are visual mediums. Why not agree that people will signal when they have something to say, instead of politely waiting (and waiting), only to be cut off by someone who's faster on the draw?

Acknowledge and celebrate success: Does the CEO's almost-imperceptible nod mean "okay"? Was he muted on another call? Or did the video just freeze? It's hard to tell. For this reason, during online meetings, it's important to acknowledge success and individual contributions, whenever possible. It may sound stupid, but virtual applause has an extraordinary impact. Andrew Lacroix, CEO of Intertek, has gone even further. Recently he told me that every day his company highlights one employee — a hero — who has introduced new and innovative thinking to his organization.

Take a walk with your colleagues. There's no rule saying a Zoom meeting has to take place indoors. Download the Zoom app and meet up with your colleagues in a field, by a lake, or in your backyard. A lack of transitions in our lives can lead to unexplained fatigue and changing venues is quite literally energizing.

Complicating meetings even more are the presence of PowerPoint presentations, known, of course, as "decks." In business, decks are pretty much the norm over the last decade or so, even though they have started to fall out of favor in recent years. As a consultant, I must confess that I typically send them to clients or colleagues in advance of a meeting. But once the meeting is underway, I only use that deck as a visual, and sometimes auditory, backdrop, only containing a couple of words and a well-thought-through illustration—a metaphor of some kind, reminding people about the essence of what I just said.

The problem is that people in meetings become enamored with these decks. What's the best way for a boss to assess an employee's productivity? Study his PowerPoint! By perusing a deck, a boss can immediately get a sense of someone's productivity. *Tom is always so incredibly well-prepared; you can tell by how long his deck is—269 slides total, with 173 graphs. Is it any wonder Tom has been promoted twice in the past year? Also, have you seen Jeanette's deck? It's 501 pages long!* In short, in workplaces worldwide, employees seem to be in an intense competition to construct the biggest, longest, most graph-filled, diagram-heavy PowerPoint deck possible.

But, seriously—as someone who spends a lot of time putting together decks and presenting them to audiences around the world—does anyone truly *get* anything out of them?

The best meetings I've ever attended had one thing in common, namely, *no PowerPoint decks*.

Why? Because when you sit across from someone in a room, the interaction becomes a dialogue instead of a monologue. (It's the same online. As soon as someone presses the SHARE SCREEN button and a seemingly endless stream of slides passes by, you can be sure half the audience is fading away as well.) With no deck present, face-to-face conversations are much more productive and useful.

One of the best meetings I ever had, in fact, was with the CEO of a global investment firm for which I consulted. We met in his office and spoke for three hours straight. There was no PowerPoint. Instead, he took fifteen pages of notes. Later, when a colleague of his and I spoke on the phone and I told her what a productive meeting the two of us had just had, the first words out of her mouth were, "Can you send me the deck?" When I told her no deck existed, she blurted out, "You just had a three-hour meeting with our CEO *without a deck*?" I could tell what she was really thinking: *How dare you waste our CEO's time like that?* and *Don't you know how we do things around here?* and *What temerity!* Honestly, for a second, I kind of felt guilty.

Instead she then said, "Well, can you *produce* a deck?"

"Sure," I said, "but you and I are on the phone, so why don't I just talk you through it? And the stuff you can't remember probably isn't important."

As I said, in my experience most people remember a maximum of three things from any deck. The rest is unimportant. Once or twice, in fact, I've done a keynote presentation where I mistakenly uploaded the wrong deck. On another occasion, 40 percent of my slides were missing. With the PowerPoint running on the screen behind me, I simply went ahead and did the keynote. Afterward, I received only a couple of emails at most, pointing out that a slide seemed to be missing. The funny thing is that the people who wrote me blamed *themselves*. Maybe they just weren't paying close enough attention? But that was it. I could have screened three hours of *Felix the Cat*, and I'll bet you no one would have noticed.

In some companies, including Maersk, I've recommended banning PowerPoints altogether. Today, the company no longer uses them, except on rare occasions, conducting most leadership meetings through tight discussion, and when necessary, a pre-digested memo form no longer than five pages.

Having said that, PowerPoints aren't an easy habit to break. It's like a two-pack-a-day smoker giving up smoking or a baby going without a pacifier. If you, or a colleague, can explain the essence of something in an alternative, more commonsensical way, why not consider skipping the whole PowerPoint thing? You won't even notice they're gone.

Is that the sun or a streetlight? Is it night yet? What time is it? What week is it? What month is it? The only thing you can be sure of is that your eyes are burning. Squinting, you can just make out the silhouette of your Zoom shirt, still hanging off the back of your office chair. Tomorrow that same shirt will be making its 128th appearance in a Zoom meeting, beginning first thing in the morning and going through to the late afternoon.

But right now, it's only common sense for you to go to sleep.

7

WHAT'S THAT LURKING IN THE SHADOWS?

AGGH, IT'S A RULE!

THERE ARE CERTAIN WORDS AND EXPRESSIONS that actually make you *feel* something. Does the word "rule" sit well with you? What about the word "compliance"? How does the word "policy" make you feel? In my experience, no three words could possibly make employees feel blanker or more stupefied.

Inside and outside companies, rules, regulations, and policies show up in a nearly infinite number of forms and disguises. That's the problem! The absence of common sense, as we now know, typically has its origins in organizational myopia, when companies begin focusing to an exclusive degree on their own internal operations and procedures — including, I might add, their rules, compliances, and policies, some wackier and less commonsensical than others.

One company I know of banned plastic water bottles — which means that the employees have to throw away their plastic bottles as they enter the office as if they were going through TSA. It gave no reason why. (Concerns about the environment, I presume?) Until 2012, Disney prohibited all facial hair and today still has a rule that male employees need to grow in their beards and mustaches, so they don't look unkempt or scraggly. Abercrombie & Fitch once issued a "Look Policy Guideline" noting that employees' hair must appear "sunkissed," with "subtle highlighting." Under S. I. Newhouse, Condé Nast — the publisher of *Vogue, Vanity Fair,* and *The New Yorker* — banned garlic from their cafeteria.

But one company brought the concept of rules to another level when it emailed questionnaires to male employees, presumably to clarify the company's stance on sex and sexual harassment.

Each question required either a yes or no answer. They included: "Have you made any sexual approaches to any fellow employees recently?," "Have you had sex recently?," and "If you did, did you use protection?" A senior officer, who'd been with the investment firm a dozen years, responded yes to the question "Have you had sex recently?" and no to the follow-up one about whether or not he'd used protection. The questionnaire, however, failed to take into account that he'd been happily married for seven years, had one small child, and was hoping for another.

After sending back the questionnaire and assuming that was the end of it, the firm's HR department hauled him in two weeks later. His questionnaire had been graded, and he'd come up short. HR told him he had to attend a daylong conduct seminar whose topics included how to use protection when having sexual intercourse. Remember: This guy wasn't eighteen years old. He was a married fifty-eight-year-old man who'd presumably ditched the condom idea when he and his wife started their family. That didn't seem to matter.

When the day came, he took a seat next to a dozen other sexual degenerates. Over the next eight hours, minus a short lunch break, he was schooled in the ABCs of sex. The format was classroom-style. What's the definition of "appropriate" sex? How often do you refrain from using a condom during intercourse? Why are condoms important? Can you name one or more sexually transmitted diseases? Do you know what HIV is? What's the best way to protect yourself against HIV? Can you get HIV by just talking to someone? This was followed by demonstrations. Everyone present was shown illustrations demonstrating how to place a condom appropriately. As the hours went on, the senior manager was called on to share his knowledge about HPV and gonorrhea, and to simulate how he might respond if he ever encountered someone who was HIV-positive. (Never mind that sex between employees in the investment firm was strictly forbidden. Explain *that*.)

Company rules, it seemed, were company rules.

The good news is that, in general, today's companies have more conventional and reasonable rules in place, ranging from bereavement and maternity leave policies to regulations concerning business travel. Except business travel rules can often cause employees no end of pain.

A well-known sticking point between companies and employees revolves around frequent-flyer points. Who "owns" those air miles, the employee or the company? Should employees be allowed to use business travel points for their own personal use? Legally, of course, having paid for the trip, the company "earned" those miles. But what about the employee who's spent after hours traveling, squashed in the back row of an Alaska Airlines flight, seated beside someone's service peacock who pecks at his knees at the first sign of turbulence? But who owns employee air miles barely hints at how emotionally charged an issue corporate travel occasionally becomes.

One company I know of offers employees the option to fly business class if the point-to-point distance exceeds 4,000 miles per flight. In this category would be, say, a flight from London to Calcutta, New York to Cairo, or Los Angeles to Berlin. The key clause here is "point-to-point." Very few airliners offer direct services from one city to another, unless it's a short hop, like Dallas to San Antonio, or Raleigh-Durham to Detroit. Most flights stop at least once, sometimes twice and even three times before reaching their final destinations. In short, those employees are not flying business class. Let's hope that they at least get to keep the air travel miles.

Another company I know has a rule that prohibits employees from even *flying* if their trip is less than 1,000 miles. Instead, they have to drive or take a train. In addition to the inconvenience, one of the company's key offices is in Ontario, on Lake Superior, the world's largest freshwater lake, meaning that employees often have to board a ferry for a hundred-plus mile journey, eating up an entire day of travel. Sadly the ferries offer no frequent sailor points.

These examples call to mind another common-sense issue I often observe in companies. Many will do everything in their power to reduce expenses while at the same time rolling out or enforcing policies that actually *increase* those expenses. Over the years I've heard countless variations of the following: an employee is hired by a company that offers to pay his travel expenses, with the stipulation that he fly economy class. Fine—he can deal with that.

The company directs him to a travel website listing all the available flights and their prices, from most to least expensive. The employee is surprised to see that the roundtrip fee to fly Economy Flexible is $3,000, whereas Business Restricted costs $2,100, a savings of nearly $1,000. The employee sees an opportunity to save his client money and also make his trip more bearable. He contacts the company, explaining the cost savings, and asks if he can pay the lower rate for Business Restricted. No, the company says, he can't. They reiterate their policy that *all employees and vendors must fly economy class.*

Apparently, the company isn't paying attention to the travel website options that are offered. Common sense would have made a difference.

Many companies also have rules that employees can only travel on one of several "approved" airlines, such as United, Delta, and Continental, presumably to save on costs. So why aren't lower-cost airliners such as Southwest or JetBlue on that same list? In a similar vein, many companies require their employees to stay at a limited, certain group of approved hotel chains. This means that if you happen to be attending a business conference in Las Vegas and none of the approved hotel chains are situated anywhere near your convention center, you have no choice but to check in at a Marriott or Embassy Suites thirty miles away, even if there's a perfectly adequate Travelodge, Ramada Inn, or Quality Inn across the street.

Another company I know sent multiple employees to a conference but stipulated that each employee could attend only one session per day. This meant the company paid for half a dozen roundtrip plane tickets from Salt Lake City to

Los Angeles, with the "savings" coming from the company having to buy only *one* day pass and badge for the conference. Some observers might wonder, *Where's the common sense?* A company would reply that a rule is a rule is a rule.

Earlier, I mentioned that company rules, regulations, and procedures can be classified as "official" or "unofficial." For as many official rules that are laid out in employee or HR handbooks, there's a matching set of unofficial rules that are tacitly upheld by managers and employees. Like family traditions, these unspoken dictates, many of obscure origin, are passed down via example and exposure, and eventually become "law."

For example, it's fair to say that most companies have official attendance requirements. Whether in person or at home, employees have to show up, in person or virtually, by 9 a.m. and leave no earlier than 5 p.m. Fine. But the unofficial and unspoken workplace rule is that if you want to get ahead in the company, it's an extremely good idea to work at your desk until 7 or 8 p.m. and continue working over the weekend. Also, that boss of yours, the one who tells everyone in your office to ignore any emails she sends over the weekend—"I'm just cleaning up my emails; feel free to ignore my notes," she says —actually *does* want a response from you . . . within the hour.

With offices now open in Europe, a twenty-five-year-old friend of mine always takes off his watch before entering his workspace in the morning. His watch is a Hublot, an expensive Swiss luxury timepiece. Why does he remove it? Simple: his boss also wears a Hublot watch and has voiced his disapproval of younger people earning too much money. Another younger friend of mine works as an intern at a company that has a twenty-hour work rule for interns and intern-level employees. Yet no one, including my friend, would ever dream of stopping and walking out the door at twenty hours. He and his colleagues work thirty-plus hour weeks to satisfy their boss and show him they're willing to exceed and even shatter expectations. The office has a rule requiring all employees to show up at work by 9 a.m. — but *he* regularly shows up at 8 a.m., or earlier, as do several of his coworkers.

What does "flex time" really mean in a company? In the post-pandemic world, virtually nothing. Can you really take time off, have a "personal day" or a "sick day," or show up later on Wednesday mornings because your daughter has a parent-teacher Zoom appointment? If so, why are you the only one taking advantage of this runaround, and are you just imagining it or has your boss been extra frosty of late? Gradually you start to understand. Working from home means just that: You're always at home. You stay longer and longer, and begin scheduling Zoom meetings and phone calls through dinnertime. "Leaving" work when you're supposed to is for amateurs and lightweights.

Yet lost in our allegiance to rules both unofficial and official is common sense, those moments when we stop to ask ourselves whether the rules we're obeying, the regulations that we're heeding, or the procedures we're following bear even a glancing relationship to ordinary and normal human behavior. Not only that, but rules create an unnecessary amount of invisible red tape, making it riskier and even more difficult to navigate the corporate landscape. In my experience, it's hard enough as it is.

• • •

One of the biggest issues in companies today centers around security, that is to say, who gets to go in and out of corporate offices. I recently visited a client at their corporate headquarters. "Hi," I said to the receptionist, "I'm here to see . . ."

She cut me off. "Sign in," she said and pointed to a nearby screen so large it almost blocked her head. More and more of these screens have been showing up in company lobbies, typically in fancier American companies all across the United States. This screen, like the others, apparently exists to funnel page after page of company rules, regulations, and policies down visitors' throats. *I'm just here for a harmless meeting in a meeting room,* I thought. *Why in the world do I need to know all this stuff?* Nevertheless, I kept scrolling, and after scanning what felt like twenty pages, I was asked to check a box confirming that I understood what I'd just read and sign my name with my fingertip, meaning my signature looked like it was written by a drunken bee with a black marker taped to one wing. The screen accepted this sloppy mess. I could now head upstairs, right?

Uncertain about what role the receptionist played, I said, "Okay, all set, I'm all checked in."

"Fine."

Silence.

"So," I said after a moment or two had gone by, "are you going to call the person upstairs?"

Actually, no, she wasn't. The huge screen was evidently so clever that once it digested my incoherent mess of a signature, it automatically emailed the executive I was visiting. Well, I knew for a fact the executive was already in the meeting and wouldn't be checking her inbox, but when I mentioned this to the receptionist, her only response was, "Just wait."

Does anyone actually read questionnaires? Whenever I go for a massage and the form asks if I'm pregnant, I sometimes check the "yes" box. No one ever notices. Perhaps I *am* pregnant!

Wait for what? What exactly was her role here? With no other alternative but to wait, I took a seat. Ten minutes later, apparently, the receptionist received a call, asking if I was in the lobby. Her body language made it obvious she had no idea if I was the visitor in question. Deciding to be proactive, I stood up and volunteered my name. She glanced up, slightly irritated by the interruption, and said to the person on the phone, "There's someone down here who says his name is Martin; is he the person you're asking about?"

I *thought* it was fairly obvious—there was no one else around—but maybe it wasn't.

Soon the security door opened, and the executive I was scheduled to meet came striding through the turnstile, her expression a mixture of apology and annoyance. "I knew you would end up getting stuck down here," she said. "It almost *always* happens, so I thought I'd better come down and find you in person. The system emailed my assistant, Jennifer, but she's out sick today . . ."

Together, we snuck past the receptionist and upstairs to our meeting.

Common sense, anyone?

Another office, another city. As usual, I was going to a meeting, and finally I found the building where it was taking place. Passing through the doors, I ran smack into security, which seems to have a ringside seat inside every corporate lobby on the planet today. First, a guard wants to see your ID. Next, you have to write down your first and last name, and then print it, followed by the name of your company; your cell phone number; your time of arrival; the name of the person you plan to meet; your car's license plate number; the time, the date, and the year; and how many polyps the doctor found during your last colonoscopy.

Still, if you take the time to look closely at who else has signed into this building, you'll discover a lot of people just blow this whole inquisition off. In one ledger I found the name "Mickey Mouse," and someone else had written "Jesus." Flip through the pages and you'll find that the late Michael Jackson, Donald Trump, and Lassie had all paid recent visits to the company. It boggles my mind the stuff you can put inside a visitor's log without anybody noticing. (Whenever I go for a masked massage and the form asks if I'm pregnant, I check the "yes" box. I do this because I'm curious if anyone takes the time to read these things or notices. No one ever has. Perhaps I *am* pregnant!)

After entrusting the ledger with all your personal details, a guard hands you a visitor's pass and ushers you through a metal detector. If you have a purse or a briefcase, those need to be screened too.

Be forewarned: things can get even more complicated if you're in possession of any "data."

Security around data, and the exchange of data, can take a lot of forms. Of course, these policies reflect corporate preoccupations with security and the paranoia around ubiquitous malware. In some companies, visitors need to first log on to a guest network with a special passcode sent to their phones and then download a program to their computers from the company network before they can even *think* about broadcasting their presentations. But corporate data security can get even weirder than that, as I found out when I was working for another global investment firm.

As part of my consulting work, I needed to send my client a PowerPoint deck (and forgive me, because I know exactly what you're thinking), a pretty fat one too — 49 MB in all. I was told that this was impossible. The firm's data security system prohibited a file that size from being sent via email. "What should I do then?" I asked. Surely the company had dealt with this issue before, right? After conferring, the staff asked me to copy my PowerPoint deck on to a memory stick and then send it to the investment firm via regular mail. I did, and it arrived a week or so later.

But there was a problem. The memory stick wasn't encrypted in the right way, and regulations prevented anyone at the investment firm from opening or downloading the enclosed file, which, I should add, was a presentation about branding that, I should also add, originated from *me*, not the firm, so it wasn't as though it was at risk of sharing its most closely held secrets with the world. Reminding me they also prohibited file hosting services like Dropbox, the company came up with another solution: Why didn't I just email my presentation? I reminded the client that it was the one who told me I *couldn't* do that. The file was large and would no doubt exceed attachment limits. The staff told me to go ahead and send it, but first I should break it down into smaller files.

I did what the employees said, sawing up the PowerPoint into 5 MB chunks and sending them the first five installments. A few seconds later, an auto-message appeared in my inbox, followed by four others, telling me that files this size were prohibited, and as a result, my emails had never reached the recipient. I then chopped up the files to 3 MB and resent them. They were rejected. I condensed them to 2 MB. Again, they were rejected, and so were my 1 MB files. In a burst of inspiration, I sliced a few pages from the 1 MB file, so it was 999 KB. This time it went through.

This meant I had a long and incredibly tedious day ahead of me. Have you ever tried to break down a 49 MB Power-Point presentation into a bunch of files no larger than 999 KB? It means you have to send out fifty emails in a row. For the next two hours, my colleagues and I did just that, whittling down the presentation into tiny crumbles, which we emailed, one after another. The good news was that the client received them. The bad news was that there now seemed to be an additional problem.

Upon receipt, the client began assembling the different small slices into a more orderly whole. But seven emails were missing. Were they too big? Had a virus done away with them? Hard to say. But they had vanished, so naturally I sent them again.

This, the second batch, never made it to the investment firm either. Forty-eight hours later, someone told me what had happened. Apparently, the seven missing files had contained banned words, and were auto-removed. *We regret that certain of your content contains inappropriate language, subject to our policies,* an auto-reply scolded me. *What* inappropriate

language? Could you be more specific? The auto-removal
message didn't say. It was like your mom crossing her arms
tightly and saying, *If you don't know, Mister, I'm not going to
tell you.*

I called the firm's IT department, and soon found myself
forwarded to an outsourced department in India. Unfortunately, the company's employee confidentiality regulations
prohibited anyone from shedding any additional light on the
matter. "But I'm not an employee," I said. "I'm a supplier." I
was told it didn't matter. Evidently whatever inappropriate language was found and flagged gave internal offense to
someone or *something.*

By now, feeling slightly psychotic, I riffled through every
single one of the twenty-nine accompanying slides in question, looking for the slightest hint of naughtiness. Nothing
even came close. I mean, we're talking about a *presentation at
an investment firm.* By this point, I'd convinced the client to
launch an informal investigation into what had happened to
those seven missing emails. In the meantime, I rewrote each
of the slides in question, and re-sent them, using a fax machine this time (amazed, by the way, that fax machines still
existed). Three weeks later, the firm's internal investigation
squad told me someone had found the inappropriate words
that prevented those seven files from going through. In no
particular order, those words were: "race," "black," "white,"
and "ban."

Taken out of context – which they clearly were – I could see
how the firm might wrongly assume I was about to somehow
start a race riot. The truth was that the presentation involved
an assessment of whether or not the firm should consider becoming a sponsor of Formula 1, the European equivalent to

NASCAR in the United States, and the world's biggest car *race*. The firm's signature colors included *black* and *white*, and the deck also questioned whether using alternative colors might be *banned* by the company itself.

Yes, you read that right: the firm *banned the word "ban."*

That's not the only word that companies (and some governments) have attempted to

> It's a fairly safe bet that the longer and more complex someone's job title is, the more bureaucratic and less commonsensical the organization probably is.

eliminate. Davio's is a chain of Italian-inspired steakhouses throughout the United States. The CEO, Steve DeFillippo, has taken it upon himself to ban the word "employee." Quite simply, he dislikes it. Its absence, he claims, motivates his team. Apple also prohibits the use of certain words in its stores. Your computer hasn't "crashed." It has "stopped responding." Your software doesn't have a "bug." It has an "issue," a "condition," or a "situation." Also, even if your laptop is so hot that flames are shooting out from it, there's no such thing as an Apple product that's "hot." Instead, it's "warm." Tell that to the firemen when they show up!

Distorted language is an increasing problem in government. At the Centers for Disease Control, employees have been told to avoid certain words, including "fetus," "transgender," "evidence-based," and "science-based." The Environmental Protection Agency no longer makes reference to "climate change" on its websites, and its scientists are no longer allowed to present scientific studies focused on that topic.

In contrast to eliminating words, the world's workforce

> One Norwegian insurance company, DNB, goes so far as to track employees' bathroom breaks. If an employee doesn't return to his desk after eight minutes, a flashing light alerts their managers that they are abusing the call of nature.

has come up with multiple variations of old jobs, slightly tricked up to sound like more than they actually are. In the past two years I've been keeping a list of new job titles whose meanings, at first, I really didn't understand. One company, for example, employs an "optical illuminator enhancer" to clean office windows. I *think* that's a window-washer. In another company, someone in HR made reference to the organization's "director of first impressions," which I guess is another way of saying "receptionist." I've also heard about beverage dissemination officers (bartenders) and a job opening for an associate to the executive manager of marketeering and conservation efforts (marketing assistant). It's a fairly safe bet that the longer and more complex someone's job title is, the more bureaucratic and less commonsensical the organization probably is.

The topic of security would be incomplete without mentioning the subject of bathroom breaks. In the Indian offices of a global company where I consult, as well as elsewhere, employees need to "clock out" and "clock in" whenever they go to the bathroom. The company is generous enough to allot two "free" minutes to its workforce, twice a day, but if employees exceed this incredibly generous allowance, their manager is notified and their time clocks are subtly adjusted. This is similar to one Norwegian insurance company, DNB, which tracks employees' bathroom breaks. If employees don't return to their desks after eight minutes, a flashing light alerts their managers that they are abusing the call of nature. Norwegian unions are rightfully appalled.

Still, none of this compares to an obscure new bathroom-related phenomenon in companies that are apprehensive about allowing visitors access to their buildings. This happened to me only once, but I'll never forget it. It involves following a guest (that is to say, me) to the men's room.

Not offering directions to the bathroom. Or pointing the way to the bathroom. Or ushering someone to the bathroom. Or smiling and murmuring, "Go down the hallway, it's the first left." I'm talking about someone actually *shadowing me to the bathroom.*

A few minutes before it happened, I was in a meeting room, surrounded by seventeen corporate executives. I'd finished my part of the three-hour-long presentation, and my client was halfway through her portion, when I discreetly stepped out of the room, intending to pay a quick visit to the bathroom. At least I *thought* I was being discreet. As I was heading for the men's room, I heard rapid, urgent footsteps behind me. It was my client. "I'll be right back," I said. "Just stealing out for a quick bathroom break." But she kept following me. "I thought you were presenting," I said over my shoulder. "I was," she said, "but I can't leave you on your own if you're going to the bathroom."

I might add the two of us were on an infinitely long floor,

with hundreds of meeting rooms, one after another, on both sides. I didn't understand. Did I need help with my zipper? Did she need to remind me to wash my hands afterward? Were there bad people hiding in the stalls?

"Wait," I said. "We trust each other, right?"

"Of course we do," she said. "But my colleagues . . ." If she didn't escort me to the bathroom, she said, one of her coworkers would probably flag her. "That's the weirdest rule I've ever heard," I said and also thought, but didn't say, *which makes this one of the weirdest companies I've ever been in.* Together the two of us, like a warden escorting a prisoner, made our way in silence along the long corridor. When I entered the men's room, as the door closed, I caught sight of her standing outside at attention. I have to confess I felt a little rushed. Afterward, she and I walked back the way we came.

When we finally got back to the meeting room, everyone was on their phones, not wanting to show, maybe, that my effort to slip out discreetly and go to the bathroom had been a big fat bust.

Somehow, in our modern, corporate world, going to the bathroom has fallen out of favor with common sense.

8

FEAR AND LOATHING IN THE CORPORATE WORLD

I'VE WORKED FOR A TON OF FINANCIAL INSTITUTIONS across the world, and two years ago, when I was working for one in Scandinavia, a senior banker asked me if I had a few moments to chat. Did I *really* want to know what this company was all about? We went into his office, I closed the door, and he started talking.

A few months earlier, he told me, he'd hung some artwork that one of his children made on his office wall. It was a crayon drawing of a dog and a train. (Or was it a horse and a train? Hard to tell.) After a multiday business trip, the banker returned to work early one Monday morning to find large code-red emergency-level block letters covering his child's drawing: YOU ARE IN VIOLATION OF GROUP POLICY. ALL OFFICE DESKS MUST BE LEFT CLEAR, WITH ALL PERSONAL AND WORK-RELATED ITEMS STORED SECURELY IN YOUR DESK BY THE TIME YOU LEAVE

WORK. PLEASE ENSURE YOU ADHERE TO GROUP POLICY IN THE FUTURE.

The banker was enraged. He was also completely baffled.

What was the firm's possible rationale for doing this? Did displaying kids' drawings serve as a kind of gateway drug, leading to employees hanging darker, more hallucinogenic stuff? A calendar of naked firefighters? Wild teenaged ponies mating on the beach? Was privacy the issue? Was hanging a child's drawing on an office wall seen as indiscreet, in an industry known for its caution and circumspection?

When I spoke to someone in HR about this incident, it turned out that no rule existed prohibiting employees from hanging personal drawings in their offices. But the thing was that just about everyone who worked at the bank *believed* that there was, so much so that it had become unofficial corporate law. Strangely enough, a lot of employees who thought the rule sounded ridiculous told me, "I knew it all along—though I never bothered to check," and employees who thought the rule was real said, "I had a funny feeling it couldn't possibly be true, but I didn't want to say anything."

It's curious how common sense was bypassed along the way.

I was consulting for this same investment firm when another issue came up: a wealthy, older female client with multiple accounts, who had been a loyal customer for decades, had forgotten to cover a monthly maintenance fee. As a result of this omission, the firm bounced a half dozen of her checks —payments, I might add, that were linked to the seventieth birthday party she was hosting for herself and that ended up causing enormous embarrassment in front of her wealthy friends. The bank might as well have accused the woman of being a grifter.

It wasn't the first time I'd heard a story like this. But where is the common sense — and consideration — that a company should show toward a seventy-year-old customer who's been with the same firm for nearly forty years? What sort of "customer care" message does freezing a client's accounts send?

All across the world, "compliance" has become an excuse to protect the status quo and ensure organizations remain in place. To not *do* things — or follow common sense. Along with legal, compliance has become a scapegoat justifying the absence of change or innovations in organizations. *Compliance will never approve that,* people say, or *Legal will definitely say no to that.* It's among the panoply of dumb laws we instinctively follow without even thinking about them or wondering why they exist in the first place because we're so scared what will happen if we don't. In this way, fear permeates an organization. The more apprehensive employees are of making a single misstep, the more fear accumulates in their minds and the more hypervigilant they become. Does anyone really want to risk failing or looking like a fool, or being humiliated or punished, or losing their job or reputation?

We habitually ignore other "laws," after all. For example, a law is still on the books in Gainesville, Florida, that makes it illegal to eat fried chicken in any way but by hand. It's against the law to play cards in Alabama on Sundays. In Carmel, California, it's illegal for women to wear shoes more than two inches high and with a base of less than one square inch. Evidently this is to keep stiletto-wearing women from catching their pointy heels in a sidewalk crack, falling, suffering

> All across the world, "compliance" has become an excuse to protect the status quo and to ensure organizations remain in place. To not *do* things.

a concussion, and then suing the city. And in Georgia, if your child is younger than twelve, you as a parent are not allowed to sell him to the circus. This means that your young son or daughter is forbidden to work as a clown, contortionist, or trapeze artist. It's just not fair!

Organizations are the same way. There are rules on the books of uncertain provenance that everyone follows because ... well, because they follow them. Almost no one knows how those rules got there, since organizations rarely keep a centralized databank of all their policies. At the same time, if you breach a company rule, you risk being disciplined or even dismissed. (In today's world, you'll *never* get fired for obeying or enforcing rules.) It's like walking on a beach, knowing that countless unexploded landmines are buried beneath your bare feet. No one knows exactly where they are. But everyone agrees you have to watch where you step.

Compliance generates fear — and knocks out common sense. Moreover, by obstructing progress and innovation, fear-based cultures don't even work. Yes, managers exist for a good reason: to hold employees accountable to timelines, budgets, productivity, and KPIs. Oftentimes they do this by holding the threat of punishment over employees' heads. But when our brains are consumed by fear and anxiety, the truth is, we don't perform at optimal levels. Just the opposite, in fact. We perform better in environments where we feel "psychologically safe."

In a 2014 TED Talk, a Harvard professor gave a concise

definition of what that means. "Psychological safety," said Amy Edmondson, is "a belief that one will not be punished or humiliated for speaking up with ideas, questions, concerns, or mistakes." In business, that means a culture where employees can speak honestly and transparently about everyday problems without fear of punishment or reprisal. The *Harvard Business Review* takes it further. "Psychologically safe environments not only help organizations avoid catastrophic errors but also support learning and innovation."

This comes as no news to Google. In 2012, the company launched Project Aristotle, analyzing 180 Google teams to determine why some succeeded and others didn't. A multitude of diagrams and thousands of hours of research later, an answer remained out of reach. Then the Project Aristotle team chanced upon Edmondson's work. In a psychologically safe workplace, said Edmondson, there's "confidence that the team will not embarrass, reject or punish someone for speaking up . . . It describes a team climate characterized by interpersonal trust and mutual respect in which people are comfortable being themselves." As the *New York Times* concluded, "Google's data indicated that psychological safety, more than anything else, was critical to making a team work." Compliance laws, it can be argued, create just the opposite effect.

To be fair, all businesses have controls and processes, and oftentimes they're in the best interest of clients, companies, and owners. Compliance is essential in the finance and banking industries, where it serves as an internal watchdog, ensuring that the institution observes industry and governmental laws and regulations. Among other things, the role of compliance is to keep an eye on possible money laundering and tax evasion while eliminating any possible future liability on the part of the bank or brokerage firm. As mergers and acquisitions multiply, compliance has gotten more complicated. If one compliance department is dense enough, combining it with a second one, followed by a third, creates a complete nest of snakes. Unfortunately, compliance and legal have almost become businesses unto themselves, with the authority to say yes or no to justify their very existence – and to keep any innovation (or common sense) from ever taking place.

The finance industries are particularly restrictive. It's all about the security of your computer. No ports, no portability. No attachments allowed. Absolutely no outside access. Long before COVID hit, when people had the option of working remotely, one company I know of had a zero-tolerance policy about employees working from home. As a result, when an employee had to take time off for a routine doctor's appointment, he often had to take off the entire day. The company didn't seem to realize that certain *kinds* of work – status meetings and reporting, researching, admin, etc. – were, in fact, perfectly safe to do from home. How easy would it be to write this into company policy if the company bothered to analyze it from a commonsensical, and not a litigious, perspective?

(One global investment firm I know had a policy warning clients that the bank was about to investigate them for money laundering, which is a little like texting your neighborhood cat burglar to hurry up and grab the jewelry because the cops are on their way.)

In this same global investment firm, employees were told that they would face disciplinary action if they used any cloud-based system to discuss internal policies. But to ask people (who after all aren't paid to be technology experts) to know if and when they're using a cloud-based system? It was as if the firm were punishing its own employees for their digital naiveté while scaring the pants off them that they would lose their jobs if they accidentally breached company policy. The result? A paralyzed organization.

In this same organization, someone had created a mailing policy that lacked common sense. If you were mailing something to the corporate office, the address of the recipient has to appear *inside* the envelope, not outside. This made no sense, since the envelopes were placed inside thick cardboard FedEx envelopes. How could it possibly matter *where* an address was printed if the envelopes in question were enclosed within thick cardboard FedEx sleeves?

Another regulation at the same firm was almost mind-boggling in its inanity. If you worked in one particular department, you weren't allowed to contact a client unless that client contacted you first. Imagine that you notice that your client, whose credit card charges typically show charges from Amazon and Apple, suddenly seems to be running up thousands of dollars in debt on gambling and yachts in southern Spain? You know her credit card has been hacked — and no doubt her credit card company has been in touch with her — but you can't contact her! What you can do, however, is get in touch with a colleague who works outside your department and have *that* colleague call the client and tell her to call *you*. Worse, once that policy was held up as a pluperfect example of the lack of common sense at the firm, the employee behind the rule admitted it was a terrible, poorly considered policy — but said he "didn't have time" to get rid of it. In other words, it's often harder to eliminate a nonsensical policy than it is to implement one. And why is this? Because everyone in the company is terrified that if a policy disappears and something goes wrong, then they will shoulder the blame. The insanity of how organizations lose their common sense can be almost hypnotic to watch. Like watching a slow-motion train wreck.

One of the sorriest examples of this happened in India, when I was working with the local Nestlé office to help the company reinvent its package design for infant formula. I soon found out that in India, there's a rule that when a company like Nestlé launches a new product and someone sues them, the CFO and legal team are personally liable for any financial penalties. *Personally liable!*

This meant that if a baby got sick eating infant formula and the family sued Nestlé and won, the payout could potentially bankrupt not Nestlé but members of upper management. Was it any wonder then that Nestlé in India, which had been trying to innovate into expanding markets for a long time, rejected 95 percent of all new ideas?

Compliance also bears the blame for today's bureaucratic hysteria around *safety*.

Few buzzwords, especially post-COVID, trigger more fear inside — and outside — organizations than "safety." The word has even crept into our hellos and goodbyes. *Safe travels. Safe journey.* Instead of — oh, I don't know — *Have a good trip,* or *Enjoy the rest of this beautiful day!* I'm not kidding when I say I've had interminable conversations with company employees about where I should place my cup on the table (otherwise it might spill, you see, causing the water to drip down the table edges, potentially affecting the electrical system and igniting a conflagration); why I should always use two hands, never just one, to hold my laptop; and why it's unsafe to spend time alone in an office after-hours. Not only does this make everyone aware that they're always in danger in any situation, no matter what they do, *safety* eliminates *any* wiggle room.

"Safety is our priority" was even the company motto of one Fortune 100 company I worked for. It was written on the wall in block letters. You weren't allowed *to use a stapler* in the company without first putting on protective eyewear. Safety, I ultimately discovered, was also the excuse the company's senior leaders used when they didn't know how to say no to your face.

Before every meeting — and I mean *every* meeting — a representative spent seven to ten minutes reading off the company's safety regulations. The rep told me where all the entrances and exits were, and what to do in the event of a fire. I was reminded to grip the handrails tightly whenever I went up and down the staircase, unless I took the elevator, and in the event the elevator was stuck between floors, then . . .

Really? This was a joke, right? It *had* to be. I sat there, motionless, waiting for the people around me to dissolve into helpless laughter. *You silly Dane!* But the faces in the room were stone. Safety was so entrenched in the company culture that one day when one of my colleagues was on a call with senior management as she was on her way to the airport, she heard suddenly, "You are in a motor vehicle right now, using hands-free audio, is that correct?" Yes, my colleague said with a laugh — *busted!* The dead-serious voice on the other end told her it was against *company safety regulations* to use hands-free technology in an automobile during a meeting. "Park your car now," he ordered. My colleague had no choice but to pull over into the breakdown lane, where she remained until the meeting ended and no one could hear her scream.

The topic of safety came up again when I arrived early for a meeting at the offices of a major oil company in Aberdeen, Scotland. Now, employees have to be extraordinarily careful when they're working on oil platforms, but the company's preoccupation with safety had seeped into and infiltrated its onshore life too. As I sat there, a company receptionist approached me. "Have you read all our safety rules?" she asked. "Rules?" I said with a laugh. "What rules?" The only reason I was there was to have an hourlong meeting. This explanation seemed to make no difference. Handing me a thick sheath of papers and a pen, she told me that once I read and understood the rules, I then needed to fill out a questionnaire attesting to that fact.

What is it about safety and stairs with these companies? I wondered. I seem to remember that I was counseled to hold tightly on to the railing when I walked up a set of stairs. That I should train my gaze downward as I ascended, while remembering to glance up every three seconds to make sure I wouldn't crash into other people who might be on the way down. That I not hold a glass of water in my hand as I walked. That if I dropped the glass and it shattered or even exploded, I risked serious injury, and for that reason I should always use a paper cup. That if for some reason I opened the staff refrigerator in the pantry to take out my lunch, I should not under any circumstances ever climb inside the fridge. Mind you, I didn't even *work* there!

Look, everybody is in favor of *reasonable* safety precautions. But at what point does common sense disappear from this picture, replaced by "business-as-usual" thinking and a collective inability to conceive of an obvious (well, to me) way out?

When I was working with Maersk, for example, the company was facing the threat of new, speedier rivals — including

Amazon—entering and potentially transforming the shipping industry. To understand how that industry operates, imagine you're a big automobile manufacturer who needs to ship 15,000 cars from somewhere in Europe, or Japan, to a port in the southern United States. Across the entire industry, this is approximately how it works:

You submit a request to a container ship operator and negotiate a freight cost. If special rates apply, your request passes through any number of departments. What's inside each container? How many containers are there in all? Do they need to be picked up and loaded? There are additional issues related to cargo, excise, and customs inspections and clearances, as well as ongoing communication with the transport system. Every country has its own byzantine laws and bureaucracies. Then there's the widespread industry phenomenon known as "rolling."

The closest analogy to "rolling" is when an airliner overbooks a flight and offers cash vouchers to passengers who agree to take a later flight. But rolling in the shipping industry is, if possible, even more gruesome than that.

Pricing fluctuates in global shipping. Companies that need their cargo shipped from one port to another typically place orders with multiple carriers. They are under no legal or financial obligation to cancel an order they made with one transporter if a second transporter offers a better price at the last minute. This means that industry operators can never be sure if a scheduled shipment will actually show up. Leaving the dock with a half-empty vessel is financially unsustainable, which is why carriers have little option but to overbook. If you're IKEA or Home Depot and your shipment gets rolled, your cargo never made it aboard the ship it was supposed to be on or it's stuck at a pier awaiting a vessel that has room for it. When the cargo finally boards, it may end up in Ethiopia or Amsterdam, as opposed to, say, San Francisco, where it was supposed to be going.

One idea I often bring to companies is a thought experiment: Can you combine two ideas in a new way? Bringing together two very different ideas doesn't always result in a groundbreaking idea, but it *does* make everyone think about their day-to-day operations in a different way. If nothing else, such an exercise stimulates creative thought.

Relatedly, I ask employees to consider how another industry that's not their own sees the world. Could they adopt *that* perspective to *their* business? Now admittedly, between you and me, this is a little like bicycling in the snow or playing tennis in the ocean — it's not *supposed* to make any sense. But that doesn't mean it can't open up a company's eyes.

For example, what would Kellogg's look like if it were bought by Apple? What would Campbell's Soup look like if it were acquired by Facebook? What would happen if Uber acquired Maersk, or if Maersk acquired Uber? Can common sense truly be applied in major industries?

If Maersk bought Uber just two years ago, I'll tell you *exactly* what would happen — and the same is true for *any* global shipping company. You would press an app on your phone to order a car to take you to the airport to catch a flight. But before the car arrived, you would have to accept and sign one hundred pages of travel waivers. An hour would go by. Next, you would have to agree to the company's terms and conditions and fill out a seventy-six-page security clearance form. You would then be asked to complete a customer satisfaction survey. By this point, you would have missed your flight, as well as the one after it, with your car still nowhere in sight. Finally, the car pulls up, but the price you were quoted on the app has increased by twenty dollars. (The cost of gasoline went up an hour earlier, and there's nothing anyone can do.)

When you're halfway to the airport, the driver orders you out of the car, since he has to make room for another passenger who has more luggage and is willing to pay more than you are. If you're lucky, another car might pick you up but with no guarantee the driver will take you to the airport—you could get dropped off at the zoo or next to a lake.

On the other hand, if Uber acquired Maersk or any other shipping company, well, let's just say that arranging for a delivery would probably be a lot easier.

When we finished this exercise at Maersk, employees realized just how slow-moving and paralyzing their industry could be. As Mette Refshauge, Maersk's vice president of communications, said to me recently, "The things people take for granted in most other businesses just don't exist in the container industry—because along with multiple systems, there are still a lot of handheld, analog processes. Our ambition was and is to create a seamless journey for the customer, one we hoped could be a huge transformation for the entire industry."

The company's new vision then became "Connect and simplify." Placing an order with Maersk had to become so simple that a child (admittedly, a very bright child) could understand it. Could Maersk minimize the number of steps customers had to go through? Yes. Would it create a revolution in the shipping industry? Yes. Would Maersk be better prepared to deal with possible disruptors? Yes.

Today, Maersk's vision—to become the "Global Integrator of Container Logistics—Connecting and Simplifying our Customers' Supply Chain"—means that if you're a client who wants to ship something from a factory, Maersk will pick it up, drive it to the dock, transport it onto a ship, and track it through to its arrival at the destination port, including loading it onto trucks and into local warehouses, all while keeping you apprised of where your cargo is every step of the way. This may sound intuitive, and obvious, but within the cargo industry it amounts to a major transformation and even revolution.

The Global Integrator strategy was simple, but its name was anything but that. What was the best way to embed a strategy promising seamless collaboration into the company's mindset? After three days huddled inside a San Francisco hotel room, company employees and I came up with what we thought was a winning concept.

Maersk would hold a *relay race* on board one of its giant ships. It would unite their entire global organization, creating a nice sense of cohesion and camaraderie. It was also an ideal metaphor for what Maersk did day after day. I proposed painting a running track on the deck of a Maersk tanker. Employees from various company divisions would take turns running and passing the baton to one another as a helicopter hovering overhead filmed the whole thing, beginning with a close-up and evolving into a wider shot showing the race was taking place on board a gigantic ship in the middle of the ocean.

Everyone at Maersk told me they loved the idea, and senior management told me it was a done deal.

But two days later, during a conference call, someone at Maersk told me there was a problem. Apparently it was impossible to film decent images from above because the view of the deck on Maersk vessels is so variable, with some sections of the boat not even visible. Ultimately the payoff just wasn't worth the expense.

But the idea didn't die there. Instead of running and filming a relay race aboard an actual vessel, we decided we would hand out *real* batons to deserving employees. Every baton is equipped with a GPS tracker, allowing us to track the spread of common sense across the world.

Whenever employees or departments collaborate cross-functionally in support of Maersk's Global Integrator mindset, the company rewards them with a baton. It's theirs, and everyone *knows* it's theirs too. We can even follow the migration of these batons on a map. As they move around the world, handed off by one heroic employee or team to the next, Maersk's success stories accumulate. Employees are encouraged, celebrated, and honored.

Unnecessary, random rules haven't just infused large corporations, they show up everywhere. Why, if you fly private jets domestically in the United States, is it not mandatory for passengers to go through security? Are you less likely to be a terrorist if you've paid more for your flight? Why is security such a big deal in airports but not if you take a train or a boat? How come *those* don't have screening machines? (I was once in an airport where a TSA officer called out, "People aged seventy-five or older do not need to take off their shoes." But why? Because there's no such thing as an older terrorist? Do terrorists retire at age seventy-five? The answer was, simply, "Regulations.") Why at the start of COVID-19 did the TSA permit airline passengers to bring aboard 12-ounce bottles of hand

Why at the start of COVID-19 did the TSA permit airline passengers to bring aboard 12-ounce bottles of hand sanitizer, while maintaining its longstanding 3.4-ounce limit for other liquids and gels?

sanitizer, while maintaining its longstanding 3.4-ounce limit for other liquids and gels?

And why is it such an ordeal to open up a bank account in Australia or to shop for shirts or travel to Canada? Let me explain.

Some years ago, I lived half the year in Australia. When I first moved there from Denmark, I was working for BBDO, the well-known advertising firm. Since the company paid my salary with a check, I went down to a local bank and said I wanted to open up a checking account. I thought it would be a snap, but it wasn't.

Australia, I learned, has something called the "100 Point System." That means that customers who want to open a bank account first need to accumulate 100 points. I was confused. "Is this . . . like some frequent-flier thing?" I asked. The customer service representative laughed. No, she said. "Then how do I accumulate 100 points?" The rep explained that if I possessed a passport, then I would automatically be awarded 100 points. "Fantastic," I said, showing her my Danish passport. "I'm sorry," she said. "That's from another country. That only counts for 35 points." "Okay," I said, "then what else can I show you?" "Well," she said, "your driver's license is worth 70 points." I showed her my Danish driver's license. "Oh, I'm sorry," she said, "but that's from Denmark, so it's only 25 points." She asked if I carried any credit cards, "since those are 25 points per card." I produced my three Danish credit cards. "I'm sorry," she said, "but those are worth only 5 points apiece."

I ended up having a total of only 75 points. "What do I have to do to get the rest of the points?" I asked. She replied that I needed to apply for an Australian passport. "Is that fairly easy?" I asked. "Sure," she said, "except you first need to have 100 points."

If this sounds overcomplicated, it was nothing compared to an experience I once had buying clothes. A couple of years ago, I went shopping for a new summer wardrobe in a Zurich department store called Globus. I found a shirt I liked and decided to buy two of them. When I approached the salesperson — a woman in her sixties — she told me the store could order the shirts and have them shipped to my hotel free of charge. First, though, I would have to sign up and provide some information — was that okay? What was my phone number? Well, I stopped using a cell phone a few years ago, and when I told her this, her face fell. "Then I'm afraid we can't deliver your shirts," she said. "Can't you just write in any old number?" I asked.

Finally, she agreed to put in the number of her office, allowing us to proceed. Then she asked for my address and zip code. "One last question," she said. "How old are you?" I told her I didn't want to answer that question. "How old are *you?*" I blurted out. She looked offended. "Why are you asking that?" she said. "Because," I said, pedaling in place, "if I'm going to get two shirts delivered to me, I just — I don't know — I just *need to know.*" Was the delivery guy intending to tell me that I'm too old to be wearing the shirt I just picked out, I went on — that my shirt would look better on a twenty-seven-year-old (which was true, I hated to admit, but still)? Is that how it worked? "We just *need* it," she said. "But *who* needs it?" I asked. "The *system*," she said. "But who or what is the system?" I asked. "I have no idea!" she said.

It goes on and on. Last year, before COVID made it impossible to cross the Canadian border, I was at LAX, about to board a plane from Los Angeles to Toronto, Canada, and from there to Seoul, Korea, with my final stop Phuket, Thailand, where I was giving a speech and had a few days of meetings. It was a twenty-nine-hour journey in all. When I got to the airline counter, the ticket agent asked for my passport and my "visa for Canada." Visa for Canada? *What* visa for Canada? I've flown in and out of Canada countless times without any need for a Canadian visa and was confused. Since when did I or anyone else need a visa to transit through any Canadian airport?

I told her that the only reason I was going to Toronto was to connect with an outbound flight to Korea. It made no difference, she said. All passengers flying into Canada needed a Canadian visa. It was a new regulation, put into place two months earlier. "But how in the world would anybody possibly know about it?" I asked. "It's on the Canadian immigration website," she replied. Of course. Like most people, nothing gives me more pleasure in my down time than scrolling through the Canadian immigration website for hour after hour. How could I have missed that?

When I told her it was the first time I'd ever heard about such a thing and that I didn't *have* a Canadian visa, she told me I couldn't board the plane. I panicked. "Well, can I *apply* for a Canadian visa? Like, right this second?" I asked. Of course, she said. Generally, it took three to five days for an application to get processed, but maybe I'd be one of the fortunate ones. I reminded her that my flight to Toronto left in exactly eleven minutes. "Well, you can certainly try your luck," she said.

Taking a seat in the lounge, I logged on to my laptop and the Canadian immigration website. A form appeared. It wanted to know everything about me. My first name. My last name. My mother's middle name. My mother's place of birth. My height and the color of my eyes. Then it asked for a list of all the countries I'd visited in the past five years.

I didn't know where to begin. In an average year, I'm in 80 different countries and 230 different cities. Per *year*. Fortunately, Signe, my assistant, on the off chance I might someday be asked this question, had created a document of all my itineraries and dates of travel, which I now cut and pasted into the form. There were now eight minutes to go before my flight left. I was convinced I'd miss it, which meant canceling a dozen appointments I'd made in the next ten days. *What is the departure time in your current time zone?* was the last question. Unfortunately, the local option, Pacific standard time, didn't appear in the pop-up menu. *Now* what? Since I was working a lot in Sydney at the time, I plugged in Australian eastern standard time, which is basically tomorrow afternoon. The form informed me sternly that I couldn't catch a flight in the past (or, it appeared, the present or the future). The closest time zone to Los Angeles was Alaska daylight time, so I selected that one. And waited. And waited. A kindly message appeared. My Canadian visa application might take several days to process, and I should remember to check my spam folder.

Four minutes to go before my flight left. Two minutes

later, a confirmation receipt appeared in my spam folder. I showed it to the ticket agent, sprinted onto the plane, and collapsed into my seat.

Laws, rules, regulations — we'd like to believe they exist for a good reason. But not when they defy our own common sense. When I began working for the Dorchester Collection, like most luxury hotels, the company was using an outside consultancy that analyzed every service moment, or touchpoint that employees had with guests. There were around one hundred of these touchpoints in all. They included moments when employees were encouraged to be "human." *Look guests in the eyes for three seconds as they approach the counter for the first time*, and *Ask guests about newspaper delivery — but make sure you don't show a religious or political preference. Formulate your request in a way that won't offend the guest or presume one newspaper or affiliation over another.*

Meaning that just because the woman in front of you looks like an East Coast liberal Democrat, don't assume she reads the *New York Times* and the *Washington Post* every morning. If guests ask for a restaurant recommendation, employees are forbidden to show any preference or favoritism. They should endorse any and all local restaurant options, and smile for at least four seconds while glancing downward and making note of the guest's selection. Okay, I'm exaggerating slightly, but am I really?

The consultancy later pored over these scorecards, looking for moments when an employee lowered her gaze after five seconds, not four, or she forgot to tell guests about room service, and added and subtracted points accordingly. If this wasn't enough to drive most employees nuts, the consultancy actually employed "mystery guests," who went around in disguise, assessing how staffers were doing when they didn't expect it. Did an employee smile enough? Did she smile *so* much it came across as creepy? Did she ask about the luggage or whether a guest needed a late checkout? And so on.

Employees were then graded and given a score, say, seventy-two points out of one hundred. Their salaries, not high to begin with, would be docked accordingly. Needless to say, the employee culture at the Dorchester Collection hotels was a little on the tense side.

Ultimately the Dorchester stopped using the consultancy and the endless checklists. It depressed morale, weakened the culture, erected a shield between employees and guests — and completely got in the way of following common sense. Just like an experience I've had too many times whenever I schedule a business lunch. Just for fun, let's go back to the same restaurant where we were shown to a table six inches away from the bathroom in chapter 2.

This time around, you and your colleagues are shown to a spot next to the window. A waiter appears and introduces himself as Scott. The table orders drinks, and when Scott comes back with them, he spends the next few minutes telling you about the lunch specials. Everyone orders and Scott says he'll get right on it.

Twenty minutes later, in the middle of a very serious group discussion, Scott comes back with your food. Setting down the plates, he takes time to tell you in detail what's in the dishes you just ordered as well as how the kitchen carefully prepared them. "Enjoy!" Scott says.

From my perspective, it's clear that you're businesspeople

having a business-related lunch meeting. That's why when Scott circles back to say, "Just checking in, guys, making sure everything is okay . . . ," instead of assuring him that things couldn't be better, one of you scowls at him and two of your colleagues just look testy. Scott doesn't seem to notice. In fact, he swings back a few more times to refill the water glasses, ask if the table could use more bread, or, his specialty, "just check in." Finally, he clears your plates, then comes back a few minutes later to ask if he can interest anyone in coffee, tea, or dessert. Oh, there are dessert specials too.

Now, I want to be clear: None of this is Scott's fault. He's really good at what he does. He's watchful, attentive to your needs, and he's doing what a waiter is *supposed* to do. But he's also following a standard script, presumably laid out in a restaurant training manual, listing the steps waiters should take to provide top-quality service and maximize their tips.

At the same time, it's also obvious — at least it is to me — that your group would prefer to be left alone to talk in peace and not be interrupted. Aren't there times or exceptions when a waiter can tell a table of businesspeople, "I can see you're having a business meeting, so I won't interrupt you. If you need anything, I'll be at the back of the room, and I'm always happy to come over"?

If I were ever offered that common-sense option during a business lunch in a restaurant, I'd eat there every day for the rest of my life.

Legal statutes and compliance laws are so ingrained in our society, and have so shunted our thinking and our behavior, that we don't even recognize them anymore. Worse, this *do-*

whatever-they-say mindset has been handed down to the next generation who, in turn, will hand it down to the following one, thereby polluting the entire business ecosystem.

Look, it's as simple as this: If something doesn't make sense, or goes against your own intuition, *say something*. The worst that can happen is that the person next to you will look up and say, "I was thinking the same thing." And the next time that person is in a similar situation, maybe he will be the one who stands up, shakes his head, and says, simply, so that everyone around him can hear it, "Y'know, that makes absolutely no sense."

9

SO WHAT COULD THE ANSWER BE?

I BELIEVE THAT EVERY GENERATION LIVES THROUGH at least one major, historic crisis, an event that has a long-lasting influence on its future habits, instincts, and behaviors. For my parents, it was World War II. For my grandparents, it was the end of World War I. Today, you and I and everyone else can tell our diaries and our grandchildren that we rode out a global pandemic whose effects are still being felt, and calculated, an experience bound to affect not just the choices we make but how we see the world going forward.

If it's true what Darwin said about the strongest species being those that are the most adaptable, what are some of the changes we might expect to see in our workplaces, and how might they affect common sense either positively or negatively?

Well, I have some bad news . . . and some good news. First, don't believe for a second that the disruptions caused by the pandemic will bring back common sense overnight. In fact, I'll bet you anything that interpersonal complexities, red tape, and other examples of bureaucratic ridiculousness have already begun making their way into your office, your bedroom, or wherever else you've set up your Zoom account, Zoom wardrobe, and Zoom bookshelves. What will change, however, is business as usual.

Two weeks into COVID-19, and it was obvious we would never work, or interact, or congregate, as we had before. A few years from now, when COVID-19 is a dim memory, many of us will still be gun-shy. We'll panic like babies without their pacifiers if for some reason we leave home without a little bottle of hand sanitizing gel. (I predict, in fact, that the airline industry will end up seeing the number of business travelers halved.) A few weeks after employees began working from home, it didn't take business leaders long to be seduced by the obvious efficiency benefits and slam-dunk cost savings arguments. From the perspective of employees, the usual boundaries between work and home that once protected their emotional lives from workplace stresses vanished as a single gigantic online channel of bureaucracy was piped straight into their homes and apartments.

Still, I prefer to look at our post-pandemic world through an optimistic lens. The changes in how we work, and the new routines most of us established have created, if nothing else, an opportunity. To wit, is there a better time in the world to abandon the nonsense of the past, reset our work routines, erase real inefficiencies, and restore common sense to our day-to-day routines?

A journey of a thousand miles begins with one small step. It's high time we took it.

Whenever I advise companies about the future, I tell executives that they need to adapt an *H2H theory*. H2H stands for "human to human." Their customers are human, not numbers on an Excel sheet, and their employees are human too. (This sounds incredibly obvious. It's not.) My goal is to chip away at the screen of detachment that isolates companies from their employees and companies from their consumers—while determining how much resistance a company has to adapt to an outsider's point of view. Banished are terms such as "B2B" or "B2C," replaced by "H2H." Whenever I'm pressed on this, I tend to give the following example: imagine that your wife sends a vase from Los Angeles to New York via FedEx, your company courier. It leaves California in one piece and arrives in New York in two hundred pieces. As a manager, you were the one in charge of selecting the workplace courier. Are you affected? Of course you are.

My overall mission? To reunite companies and their employees with their own common sense, empathy, and humanity. The five steps to getting there are as follows:

1. CAGED

"Caged" sounds like a 1950s black and white prison movie with a bullish female warden and an unjustly imprisoned shoplifter (it probably was too). Caged is also an apt description of nine out of ten companies, whether they know it or not. It's also perhaps a contributing factor to the fact that, according to statistics released in 2018 by the Small Business Administration, roughly one-fifth of all business startups go bust in the first year, half of all new startups fail within five years, and only one-third last for longer than ten years. At least half the world's companies are in a crisis — they just don't know it. My first job on site, then, is not to implement change, but activate the *need* for change.

Before we explore this further, I want to tell you about a research study I read about that involved chickens.

A team of researchers took a group of chickens and placed them inside four individual cages for six months. When they finally opened the doors, expecting the birds to dash out in search of freedom, the researchers were surprised when the chickens took a few tentative steps forward before retreating back inside their cages. So much for the Great Escape.

In the second part of this study, the research team tried to figure out how to lure the chickens out of their cages so that they stayed out. The best way, they decided, was to entice and reward the birds using corn kernels.

First, they placed the four chicken cages in a small, enclosed area. They positioned two cages on one side of the room and two cages across from them, with maybe three feet of space separating them. Now, where should they place the corn kernels? In the middle of the room, equidistant from all four cages? *Inside* the cages? Neither of these strategies worked. The chickens eyed the corn in the middle of the room but stayed where they were. They pecked at the corn inside their cages, but nothing more. The team finally positioned the corn kernels one or two inches outside of each cage. Soon all the chickens had ventured out of their cages to sample the corn. That was all it took.

To me at least, the Chicken Cage Syndrome illustrates that

small, modest changes *do* work. CEOs enjoy talking about "the big picture" (e.g., where their organization will be ten years from now), but seriously, who can possibly relate to that? The average employee spends less than five years in his job, generally outlasting both the CEO *and* the CFO. What if CEOs focused instead on where their companies will be in a year or in two years? That's a lot more relatable for everybody. The Chicken Cage Syndrome shows that common-sense changes are best carried out using small, tangible, immediately "winnable" steps. If a proposed change is too big, bold, or ambitious, the fear of the unknown is too great, and most companies (e.g., their employees) will be resistant to and reject it.

For that reason, when I begin working for an organization, one of the first things I try to do is *activate the need* for change. Where in the company is common sense most conspicuously lacking? With the goal of diagnosing the company's degree of resistance to change, as I mentioned earlier, I sit down and interview as many employees as possible.

During these interviews, I typically show employees a series of photographs that serve as unauthorized Rorschach tests. One shows a man trapped inside a narrow wall space, looking pinched and claustrophobic. Another shows a mom and a dad yelling and gesturing at a child. *Which of these photos most accurately describes how it feels to work here?* I ask. *Which photo do you think relates best to this company?* If the photo of the parents yelling and gesturing is generally agreed to describe a problem within the company, then the employees and I discuss in what ways company leadership is poorly aligned and how it can be improved. Photos not only facilitate conversation, they often show — and elicit — emotions that may otherwise be challenging for employees to express.

Typical of the kinds of follow-up questions I ask include: *What was the original impression you had of this company in your first few weeks or months? When you were first hired, what did you hope to achieve or contribute?* I also inquire about the legacy of change in the company. *Did this particular project you worked on succeed here? Why or why not?* Often I'll find that the person or team responsible for launching a change or initiative actually took a decidedly unorthodox path. They broke rules, took risks, and otherwise overturned conventional ways of thinking. I file these examples away, knowing how useful they are as models that can accelerate company behavior.

In two or three weeks, the *real* org chart of the organization is gradually revealed. I also have a vivid snapshot of how a company deals with change.

Common-sense issues tend to leap out at once, though sometimes companies are unwilling to consider making even small commonsensical or obvious changes — as I found when I met with the senior team at one of the world's largest plastic bottling manufacturers.

We were in a workshop, discussing the importance of getting to know your customers, when one of the plastics executives raised her hand. She understood the company's consumers *extremely* well, she said. This led to a conversation about plastic consumption worldwide and concerns about climate change and what factors were most responsible for environmental damage. Somewhat surprisingly, the executive placed the blame entirely on consumers. "If people want less plastic in their lives, they can just stop using plastic bottles," she said.

Taken aback, I asked her to explain her thinking. "Look," she said, "no one is *forcing* anyone to use a plastic bottle. We all have choices in life." I reminded her that in many parts of the world, water supplies were limited and that residents in some areas of Africa and Asia had no alternative other than plastic bottles. "Also, what about those individually plastic-wrapped pieces of cheese?" I said. "Is that the fault of consumers too?" "Yes," she said. "They don't *have* to buy that cheese if they don't want to!"

It made no difference what I said or how I countered. She was unwavering in her belief that consumers were exclusively responsible for the amount of plastic clogging the world's landfills and oceans. I didn't agree. *Didn't she see that her company produced plastic — in fact, a good chunk of it?* My opinion made no difference to her either. Neither of us saw things as the other one did.

That kind of non-blinking, dogmatic attitude from an executive clearly gets in the way of common sense — especially when it comes to relating to the environmental concerns of consumers.

Returning to the concept of Caged. My mission is to force companies to see themselves not from the inside out, but from the outside in. Helping facilitate this process are a few simple exercises.

In the first, inspired by industrial designer and author Ayse Birsel, I gather everyone in a room, hand out pens and pieces of paper, and ask everyone to sketch a portrait of the person sitting beside them. If this sounds easy or simplistic, you've probably never tried it. Drawing another person's face obliges you to look directly into her face, and the person who's drawing *you* has to do the same. This mutual staring contest creates an instantaneous bond of empathy, especially in a world where we're transfixed by our phones and only rarely make eye contact with others. The drawings that employees hand in are usually disastrous – everyone looks like a sea monster – but that's not the point. The goal is to increase a sense of empathy among employees.

In the second exercise, I equip employees with instant cameras and ask them to take a photograph of anything they see or experience in the company that shows a lack of common sense. It could be travel expenses that take up to two months to be reimbursed or a call center screengrab of a customer who wanted to cancel her credit card but couldn't until she filled out six different forms. Employees then post these photos on a bulletin board with a brief description of the problem – for example, *One caller had to fill out half a dozen forms and wait three weeks before we canceled her credit card.*

Two weeks later, there might be a dozen or more photos on the bulletin board. I divide them into categories. One might be No Common Sense in Accounts Payable. Another might be No Common Sense Assisting Customers-in-Crisis. A third could be Travel Approvals. Very quickly you can see where in the company daily common sense is lacking. Do you remember the TV remote control I wrote about earlier? If so, you'll also recall that the problems a company suffers from *internally* are usually mirrored *externally*.

Using the bulletin board photos, management and I then construct a fantasy of an ideal company – though before doing that, I tell them we first, of course, have to address the common-sense issues on the bulletin board.

As I said earlier, management and employees need to understand the *pain* their customers and employees experience – whether it's the marketing executive who has maxed out his credit card since the company hasn't reimbursed him

> The average employee spends less than five years in his job, generally outlasting both the CEO *and* the CFO. What if CEOs focused instead on where their companies will be in a year or in two years?

for his travel expenses or the hotel guest, cross-eyed with jet lag, who's forced to make small talk with the desk clerk.

How would an ideal company handle problems like these? What is the one word that sums up the company's mission and clearly defines what its purpose is? For Volvo, it's "safety." For Google, it's "search." For Disney, it's "magic." With the Dorchester Collection, the word was "iconic." With Maersk, it was "one-touch," a reference to the company's revolutionary new method of engaging with customers. With Swiss International Air Lines, it was "Swissness," and for Cath Kidston it was "carefree."

So what's *your* company's word? Is it "responsive"? Is it "cool"? Is it "human"? Come up with a word—and *claim* it. If you chose the word "human," aspire to be human in every one of your encounters and touchpoints, allowing "human" to guide every decision and initiative your company makes. By choosing a single word (ideally one that has an edge), you are now obliged to "raise the bar," to improve your work environment and customer interactions, while giving yourself a carte blanche mandate going forward to create a workplace where employees don't have to check in for approval all the time. In the best-case scenario, "human" becomes a self-fulfilling prophecy.

In short, get away from being Caged. Be human.

2. COURAGE

Have you ever glimpsed a neon red FIRE sign over a doorway in a school, company, or municipal building? Obviously they were designed to direct you safely out of a room in the event of combustion. The thing is, if you've ever been in a *real* fire, chances are that it's unlikely that red FIRE sign would be helpful. A room on fire usually fills up quickly with smoke. Inhabitants drop onto their stomachs, panicked, and shimmy and crawl toward the nearest exit. But where *is* the exit? The room is so thick with smoke no one can see anything. Why, then, are FIRE signs positioned over doorways, if people trapped in rooms are unlikely to see them during a fire? Wouldn't it make more sense to position FIRE signs closer to the floor, matching the perspectives of people who may be struggling to escape a fire, as a growing number of companies in Scandinavia and Japan have now done?

Different? Yes. But these companies have had the courage to challenge traditional safety concepts and have implemented common-sense approaches instead.

This second step, Courage, occurs when companies and employees begin instituting a series of small changes that yield immediate positive results. Put another way, it's when the chickens are finally lured out of their cages. This takes place during what I call the "90-Day Intervention."

Notice that I didn't say 5-Year Intervention or even 1-Year Intervention. No, I said 90 days, mirroring Wall Street's 90-day quarterly earnings schedule. Tell companies how to change and most will hear you out, agreeing that change is necessary and "good." Problem is, a few months later, enthusiasm inevitably sags. They realize they didn't *really* want to change, and they promptly revert to their default mindset.

So rather than explaining what changes I have in mind for them, I propose we simply go ahead and *do it*. By way of analogy, imagine if before you rode a bike for the first time, someone insisted you read an eighty-two-page bike manual. Odds are it wouldn't help you in the least. You need to get on the bike, wobble, pedal, wobble some more, fall, crash, get back up again, ride a few feet, and tip over again. Only then should you take the time to read the bike manual.

This strategy involves doing things quickly, accurately, and efficiently — within a 90-day time limit. A ticking clock injects a sense of urgency to the proceedings, which typically dissolves company politics. In my experience, the busier and more focused that employees are on hitting a target, the more that internal politics disappear. With only 90 days to carry out a series of small changes, who has time to be snaky or go around colleagues' backs?

Courage focuses on small, easy wins, or what I call "proof points" — company-wide common-sense issues that can be resolved quickly, the results of which immediately make life easier and better for everybody. It could be a new rule eliminating cc'ing and bcc'ing or another that says that if coworkers are seated within a twenty-foot radius of your desk, instead of calling, emailing, or texting them, you have to get up, walk over, and *talk* to them.

Why are small steps so important? Well, think back to the chickens. When the researchers placed the corn kernels in the middle of the room, the chickens froze. Nor did they respond much when the corn kernels were placed inside their cages. But when the researchers placed the corn one or two inches outside the cage doors, the chickens then ventured out of their cages—and stayed out. Between them, the chickens gave the others "permission," or even the "courage" to change.

Consider the alternative. If I handed management a long list of changes and one or two didn't work out as planned, company naysayers would use those stumbles as evidence that even seemingly insignificant changes were doomed to fail. Those small steps would become *negative* proof points. During workshops, I ask employees to brainstorm solutions for simple issues. Nine times out of ten, someone will raise their hand and propose an app. Invariably my response is: *if you can't solve this issue without using an app, in most cases it can't be solved*. Solve it manually first, and only then consider transferring it to an app. But in general, 99 percent of all problems can be solved without one.

Now, from an operational perspective, none of these small changes, or proof points, will have a profound effect on a company. But by thawing or unlocking what employees assumed was mandated corporate law, they have a powerful influence on the culture. If small changes can have immediate and positive effects, imagine what much larger changes can do.

Best of all, these changes often originate from employees you would least expect. If, during my preliminary interviews, I find that a so-called lower level employee named Jim has a brilliant idea, I immediately run it past the CEO. *Of course,* the CEO usually says. *I'm amazed that policy isn't already in place.* I then give Jim permission to implement his idea throughout the organization, which signals to him (and his colleagues) that his (and everybody's) ideas are as valuable as anybody else's. Over the years I've dubbed this the "elevator approach," as it encapsulates my belief that a company should be able to *elevate* from the bottom to the top, bypassing what I call the "frozen middle" of the organization—literally, a company's middle management, which is often overworked, squeezed for resources, lacking any mandate or incentive for change, and effectively paralyzing the organization—and disseminating immediate change all across the organization.

Next, I ask employees to imagine how someone in the company who finds the mere idea of change to be silly, or pointless, might respond. In what ways would that person push back? I have found that when employees are asked to impersonate a naysayer who has mounted a vociferous argument against change, they realize how foolish any objections sound—infusing a positive mindset into the organization from the very beginning.

A good or innovative idea is like a perfect rectangle. What generally happens to that rectangle as it passes through an organization is that its four sharp corners—representing what makes it new, fresh, or memorable—are sanded and eventually smoothed down to nothing. In the end, the rectangle ends up looking more like a circle, one that pleases everybody and therefore nobody. Are the small changes the company has agreed to implement intact rectangles—or have they been sanded down so much they now look more like rounded corners? What compromises have been made?

The employees who are leading the change need to reinforce the original concept, sometimes over and over again. They need to write it down *exactly as it was*, take note of the places where compromises have occurred, then go back, reshape, and sharpen the four corners of the original idea.

Why bother writing it down? you might wonder. Because as a company's immune system reasserts itself, minds sometimes change, second-guessing happens, the invisible red tape in employees' minds starts to blind them, and before you know it, any number of compromises has turned bold rectangle into an extremely mushy circle. Writing down an idea makes it easier to revisit it later on. You can compare your concept as it first existed and the concept as it evolved (or, more likely, devolved).

For example, a few years ago, I was asked to come up with a strategy that could help alleviate anxiety in children suffering from cancer before and during their fMRI scans. Inspired by similar challenges across the United States, my team's goal was to make these kids feel more comfortable inside those cold, fear-inducing modern machines.

We decided to replicate an environment beloved by most children – the beach, recreating an ambiance soothing enough to lessen their fear and apprehension. The base idea was simple. We would turn the fMRI scanning room into a metaphorical beach. If the concept were a rectangle with four sharp corners, it would look like this: In one corner, there was an enormous sand castle. Another corner broadcast the sounds of waves and seabirds. A third corner featured a bench with several beachy-looking plants, with a painting of the ocean over them. The fourth corner involved exchanging the sterile lab coats of the technicians for more tropical outfits.

Everyone loved the idea – *In-ter-est-ing!* . . . but . . . Martin, instead of creating a real sand castle, why don't we just paint the scanner a sandy brown color? Do we really have to play the sound of ocean waves (it will distract and bug the staff and patients)? Wouldn't it be easier to use headphones? Let's stick with the usual white uniforms and scribble funny nametags on them, like "Master of Ice Cream" — are you okay with that, Martin? *Wait,* here's an even better idea: we'll hire someone to draw a series of beach- and ice cream–related cartoons, and hand them to the children when they enter the room, they'll love it . . .

Again, write down your idea *exactly as it was* — and hold on to it for dear life.

3. CELEBRATION

By now, one or two chickens have ventured shyly outside their cages. Having spotted the corn, they're now pecking at it. The other birds look on enviously. Will they stay inside their cages or join them in this mini-feast? The only way to convince the other chickens to go forward is to provide positive modeling. The first two chickens who left their cages have come to no harm — that's for sure. They even seem to be enjoying the spotlight. Doesn't that show that it's really okay to leave the cage?

Along those lines, I find that at the start of any 90-Day Intervention, most employees are energetic, optimistic, and eager to implement changes. But after 90 days, or typically around Day 75 or Day 80, their optimism flags because either the company's immune system can't handle change or employees are being bombarded with second thoughts.

I have a theory as to why. Think about how slowly or quickly time goes by depending on where you are or what you're doing. If, say, you're on an airplane waiting to disembark and the captain breaks in to announce that one of the engines has a technical issue — *We'll get back to you as soon as we know more* — five minutes suddenly starts to feel like five hours. When transitions happen, our perceptions of time inexplicably change. Without constant, ongoing communication and evidence of change, employees will begin to feel as though nothing is happening. If, say, after 90 days the employees feel that they are working harder than management to create lasting common-sense change, they will likely begin to lose faith in the project, in management, *and* in the company.

This is why change needs to be visible at the highest levels, whether it's the CEO walking the hallways or top executives taking time to respond personally to employee emails and customer complaints. These gestures alert the company that change really *is* happening.

From a customer service standpoint, consider Inditex, the parent company of Zara, one of the world's largest clothing brands. Despite their own cutting-edge data center keeping them up to date on sales, daily and even hourly, Inditex employees still place a personal call every afternoon to every one of their retailers. This is all to say that even in the event you've identified customer service problems, don't stop there. *Visit* your customers. Film a video or take photos, and share what you've learned in weekly meetings.

Most crucially for your employees, *celebrate* your wins. Only rarely do organizations commemorate truly special occasions. If they do, these usually revolve around boring economic metrics, soaring stock prices, or a cursory email that shows up in your inbox telling you that Barb in accounting is turning fifty next week, and asking whether you will be chipping in for cake and a hot stone massage. Designed mostly to please HR or throw a bone to employees, these sorts of celebrations are often the extent of a company's recognition of the culture.

Common sense says this is simply not enough — especially when good, positive changes have been made and become proof points of hope.

Celebration is very simple. It asks companies to commemorate their small, tangible victories. Celebrating *matters*. It actually makes a difference.

Observing and celebrating small victories also reinforces the belief among employees that they're indeed playing for the right team. No matter how small or insignificant a change may appear, it holds symbolic value for the other members of the tribe. By recognizing and celebrating contributions, a company shows that management is not only listening to employees, it values them too.

Via the Celebration step, companies also anoint heroes — employees who during the 90-Day Intervention fought and prevailed against the company's very resistant immune system.

4. CHECK THE CAGE— AND CONQUER

Traditional moviemaking, at least in the West, follows a well-trod formula. Films have three acts, with the second act being the longest. In act 1, we meet the characters and are given a series of snapshots of their lives. As act 1 ends, an event happens: A husband tells his wife he's in love with somebody else. A woman moves back to her tiny, quiet hometown to tend to an elderly parent. The Godfather is shot. Act 2 advances this storyline, introducing subsidiary characters, conflicts, set-backs, and bottlenecks. Moments before act 2 ends comes the "all is lost" moment. That's when the female protagonist finds out her fiancé is in love with his best man; the marriage is off; she loses her job; she blows up at her best friend. As I said, all is lost. But then act 3 resolves these conflicts en route to a happy ending.

You wouldn't know it, but this structure is also common to all cultural transformations.

In business school textbooks from the 1970s and 1980s, change in companies happens agonizingly slowly. Charted on a graph moving from left to right, the squiggly line begins high up, signaling a company's success (and self-satisfaction), before plunging and beginning another ascent that culminates in a high point no different from where it began.

But today, graphs like these don't often make sense. Change in companies begins at the lowest point on the graph (representing low morale) and often happens rapidly. Graph lines rise, and continue rising. And just when you think the line can only go higher, three-quarters of the way to the end, it plateaus and even sinks. It's the "all is lost" cinematic moment, corporate-division.

Three-quarters of the way through any corporate transformation, a company *always* slumps. This drop takes place when a company realizes that change isn't some abstract idea or theory. It's *real*. Employees also realize, some for the first time, that *they* need to change too. With this step, Check the Cage — and Conquer, you effectively padlock all the chicken cages to prevent employees (or the chickens) from retreating and hiding out back inside. Sometimes, before you do that, you're obliged to witness a failure or two. Let me explain.

I ask employees to transform one small thing that makes their lives, their surroundings, and showing up for work every day easier or more bearable.

Once, during a workshop at one of our fashion clients, my colleagues and I found ourselves surrounded by an astounding 180 different patterns in an industry where 10 to 20 patterns is the company average. Signature designs adorned handbags, shoes, pants, rolls of wallpaper, and everything else it can think of. What was the point of having so many patterns, with many encompassing up to two dozen different colors? It was costly and unproductive. My colleagues and I convinced management to sharply reduce the number of patterns from 180 to 25. We left the workshop confident we'd made progress.

But as time went on, one of the design teams didn't change at all. Despite what we'd discussed during the workshop, the company was still using 111 separate patterns. "What about what we all talked about at the workshop?" I asked. I was told by management that one of the departments hadn't accepted our verdict. A top executive even told me to be careful about interfering in traditional processes. "If you don't stop this right now," I said, "you are giving this entire company a mandate *not* to change. You're sending a signal that change is irrelevant to the rest of the organization." Yes, in the short term, the changes we proposed might cost the company money and "interfere with processes," but in the long term the company would definitely benefit. The executive understood, made a phone call, and the problem was fixed. This is what I mean by Conquering.

Here's the thing, though: make sure you have a concrete solution ready for whatever problems come up — and that you communicate that solution to everyone in the company. If you don't, people will start talking. They'll tell everyone that change didn't happen, that change was impossible to sustain — and slowly, the chickens will find their way back to their cages, where they'll remain, gently sighing and clucking, for the rest of their lives.

5. CONTRIBUTION CULTURE

In this step, Contribution Culture, you appoint common-sense change agents — and set them free across the organization. But not just anybody!

The closest analogy to a common-sense change agent is a personal trainer who shepherds your workouts at the gym. The job of a personal trainer is to push you beyond your default levels of comfort, to encourage or even goad you whenever you're feeling lazy or hopeless, or if you're not making enough progress. They keep you from throwing in the towel when your arms hurt, you're pink in the face, and you want nothing more than to surrender and go home.

Earlier I wrote about how lower-level employees are often the ones who come up with the most commonsensical solutions to corporate problems. The company recognized our imaginary employee, Jim, perhaps for the first time, letting him briefly enjoy the spotlight. Since then, Jim has become a true believer. Other employees in the company saw what happened to him, and they want some of that attention themselves. These are the employees most likely to become designated common-sense change agents.

I usually take them aside. I ask them to transform one small thing that makes their lives, their surroundings, and showing up for work every day easier or more bearable. It could be a change in the company's calendar meeting system. It could be changing the names of meeting rooms from Room 2871LSPG9 to the Avengers Room or the Jay-Z and Beyoncé Room.

Why do I ask them to do this? Well, for one thing, they need to realize how difficult change is. If you happen to be right-handed, have you ever tried brushing your teeth using your left hand? It's an awkward, even bizarre experience. Change can be hard.

In any event, once those employees have made that single change for a month, I then ask them to present the results to the group. Then I ask them to select five individuals in the company who they either know well or like and respect. These are people who can be convinced to do things. The key role for common-sense change agents is to consistently activate the need for change — which inevitably shows up as employees discover things that run counter to common sense.

Storytelling ranks high up among the traits of the world's most admired leaders, a fact most companies forget. Still, if your mission is to inspire your employees to do something, the last thing you want to do is barrage them with numbers or statistics about how great or how poorly your business is doing. No matter how useful they are, facts and statistics target our rational brains, period. Hearing about the company's stock price leaves most of us impressed but cold. *No one* makes a decision using their rational brains. By contrast, well-told stories are *emotional*. When trying to enact change, come up with a positive and memorable story to get your point across to your employees.

Let me give you an example. In the early 1960s, President John F. Kennedy was touring NASA headquarters in Houston, Texas. When he asked one of the sanitation staff why he was there, the cleaning staffer didn't answer that he was there to survey and inspect spacecraft fuselage #4798. He said, simply, "Mr. President, I'm here to put a man on the moon."

Metaphors have a singular ability to make everyone in an organization feel as though they are all part of the same mission. No one ever questions a metaphor. If I tell you, *Lego manufactures 124 million small plastic pieces annually*, you'll be so bored you'll fall asleep before I finish saying "annually." But if I say, *Lego manufactures the equivalent of 123 million men stacked to the moon and back*, the words – and the idea – come alive. You might not be able to imagine it, but you can get behind that! As a shortcut to emotion, metaphors can be used to translate intangible things into tangible ones. Is it any wonder that Lego's new mission statement is "Inspire and Develop the Builders of Tomorrow"?

This is why I train employees in and encourage storytelling – including "elevator pitches," in which they have a minute or less to summarize a story or a process. In the end, they learn to tell engaging stories that hit the nail on the head about common sense, stories with which everyone in the company can empathize. Not sympathize, *empathize*.

People begin smiling again. They start to really, truly believe in what they are doing. Ready or not, they're poised for the final step, which is to establish a Ministry of Common Sense in their own organizations.

10

IMPLEMENTING THE MINISTRY OF COMMON SENSE

YOU DID IT. YOU LEAPFROGGED OVER YOUR boss, and your boss's boss — an almost inconceivable act of rebellion — and now you're on your way to meeting your company's CEO.

Farewell red tape. Goodbye 24/7 production line, the one that yields one idea lacking in common sense after another. You're about to make things *happen.*

You climb on to the executive elevator, and a few moments later the doors part to reveal a still, spacious carpeted expanse. It's like Heaven up here. If a cherub grazed you with her wing tip and flew away, you wouldn't be surprised. Your shoes make no sound as you pass by a series of executive personal assistants and are greeted, finally, by executive personal assistant number one, who welcomes you warmly, offers you bottled water, and invites you to take a seat. The CEO is in a meeting, she says, but he'll be out shortly.

As you sip your water, you gaze around you. On this floor,

worries seem to have been bought off. Everything works, flows, joins, gleams, coordinates, makes sense. The art is tasteful, the row of conference rooms empty, spotless, glass-windowed, and apparently uncontaminated by human life. And if a laptop screen even *considers* freezing or flinching — which seems unlikely — a dedicated IT department is standing nearby, like the Queen's Beefeaters.

There's only one problem you can anticipate: How do you convince a CEO who lives up here in Heaven, and almost never passes through the purgatory where you and your colleagues spend all day, that common sense is lacking in his company?

A few minutes later, you're ushered into the CEO's office. You explain the issues around common sense that have recently come to your attention. The CEO listens attentively and nods briskly. *You know, that's a perfect job for Rob.*

Oh no. Anyone but Rob. Rob, middle-aged, portly, golf-obsessed, and severely ADHD, is the walking, wheezing incarnation of the lack of common sense in this company. *Rob* is on the job? Your *cat* could do better. Your *cat's tail* could do better.

You leave the office with your head down. The CEO might as well have said, *Send me a deck,* or *Makes sense — let's integrate this into our existing workstream.*

In your heart, you know nothing will happen. And unless you create a Ministry of Common Sense in the company, chances are nothing will keep happening, over and over again.

The last step of the change process involves creating a "governing body" to systematically vacuum up the lack of common sense in your company and replace it with simple, intuitive

> A Ministry of Common Sense ensures that the daily, common-sense solutions that a company has already committed to creating aren't made out of duct tape, frayed string, and bent safety pins — that real change will last, without compromising the business or its employees going forward.

solutions that eliminate confusion and impracticality from the lives of both employees and customers. This governing body is otherwise known as the Ministry of Common Sense.

I can imagine what you might be thinking. *You expect my company to appoint an actual Minister of Common Sense?* C'mon, *a Ministry of Common Sense will never happen, not in* my *company.*

When I tell senior leadership teams that the best way to guarantee ongoing common sense in their companies is by establishing a Ministry of Common Sense, their lips twitch. They nod. They wait for the punchline, for the moment when I cry, *Ha! Ha!* They assume I must be speaking metaphorically. I couldn't possibly believe that *any* serious company would ever allocate the resources to fund a position focused exclusively on illuminating and untangling corporate misalignments, miscommunications, inefficiencies, and all the rest.

Well, I do.

By now I hope it's clear that common-sense lapses in companies typically escape the notice of the people who work there. Common sense tends to be a blind spot, something misplaced by individuals as they go about their everyday business. Employees are often so internally focused that they don't even notice that what they're doing makes little practical sense to anybody outside the organization.

As such, establishing an actual Ministry of Common Sense ensures that the daily, common-sense solutions that a company has already committed to creating aren't made out of duct tape, frayed string, and bent safety pins — that real change will last, without compromising the business or its employees going forward.

Imagine that your organization has just been through the five-part process I described in the last chapter. Everyone is now going around talking about the Chicken Cage Syndrome and how to avoid Rounding the Corners. Here and there things have definitely improved. But life and business move fast. Industries and businesses change. New technologies move along. Employees come and go. Institutional memories are spotty, and corporate amnesia and inertia can overtake any organization if it's not vigilant. It's easy to slip. Before anyone knows it, and despite everyone's best efforts, the business pivots away from common sense once again. Company inboxes swell with hundreds of emails, no one can get their travel itineraries approved in a timely manner, and executives have resumed saying "Send me a deck" without breaking stride.

What I'm proposing is that the Ministry of Common Sense is best framed as a prophylactic — a first defense move against a company sliding backward into old, bureaucratic habits, practices, routines, and perspectives. It's also a way to catch problems or inefficiencies *as* they happen. Appointing a Minister of Common Sense also sends an unmistakable signal that a company values its employees and takes common sense seriously enough to be on the lookout, full-time, for its absence and for when it needs to be applied. But let's also be realistic. What company has its act together enough to set up a department tasked with redressing the things that impede common sense? How would that even work?

To answer that question, let me introduce you to Chester (not his real name), a nearly twenty-year-veteran of a giant global investment firm I worked for, who took it upon himself to set up the company's first-ever Ministry of Common Sense.

Chester and I met during a workshop in San Francisco. I was encouraging the company where he works to set up a Ministry, and the response, I remember, was extremely positive. But then a month passed. No one ran with the idea. Everyone seemed to be waiting for someone else to broach the topic. A few weeks later, Chester contacted me. Things had come to a head for him recently, he said, when a senior executive had "shadowed" him for twenty-four hours in an effort to understand what day-to-day life was like for middle managers. For both Chester and the senior leader, the experience was illuminating.

The executive who spent a day following Chester around was named Perry. Chester had known Perry for years and considered him a friend, which is why when Perry encouraged Chester to be blunt and share his complaints about the company, Chester promised he would hold nothing back. "Actually," he said to Perry, "if you're serious about seeing what it's *really* like to be me, and work for this company, why don't *I* decide how we spend the day?" So instead of meeting at the office, he told Perry, they would be catching a flight to Denver early the next morning. Chester had already booked his ticket on a flight leaving San Francisco at 6:05 a.m. Per company policy, it was the cheapest available flight. He forwarded his travel information to Perry's office.

An hour later, Perry's office called to let Chester know that the airline he had chosen "didn't work for Perry" — it seemed Perry had frequent flyer miles with another airline. The office proposed that the two men take a later flight that left at a more reasonable hour, say 10 a.m. "That's actually a disciplinary offense in this company," Chester replied. It didn't matter where company employees flew or who they planned to meet there. Company regulations required them to take the cheapest flight available, no matter what time it left or how many stops it made. Reluctantly, Perry's assistant reserved a seat for her boss on Chester's 6:05 a.m. flight.

The next morning, the two men met at the airport. As Chester headed over to the economy line, Perry looked embarrassed. "I should point out that I'm flying business."

Chester reminded Perry that per company policy, all company employees, even senior management, had to fly economy — and that if for some reason Chester were tallying up disciplinary infractions (which he wasn't), this would be the second policy regulation Perry had broken. It was barely 6 a.m.

Soon they were airborne. Chester had told Perry to stay in his seat in business class until Chester came to get him. There was no in-flight Wi-Fi and when Chester met up with Perry in the front of the plane, he noticed that Perry had just turned on his cell phone. "You know, I really hate to say this," Chester said, "but you and I aren't allowed to use our phones until we get inside company offices and are using the secure corporate Wi-Fi network."

"But I need to get my emails," Perry said.

"Hey, I do too," Chester said, "but the thing is, neither of us are legally permitted to go online until we get to the office. It's company policy." Chester added that sometimes this meant that after his flight landed, he waited up to ninety minutes to use his phone in the company office, despite the fact that clients and team members relied on his quick access and availability.

As they took a taxi to the company's offices in downtown Denver, Perry grew more and more silent. "Are you paying for this?" Perry asked Chester when they arrived. "I can't," Chester said, explaining that even if he was willing to pay the taxi fare, he couldn't, per company policy. As a non-senior employee, he wasn't allowed to pay a taxi fare if a senior executive was also a passenger in the cab — "the only exception being if my life were in danger somehow, which of course it's not." When Perry realized he had no cash on him, just credit and debit cards, he had another idea: Why didn't he just shoot an email to Chester, authorizing him to pay the fare?

"That won't work," Chester said. "Remember, neither one of us is allowed to go online or send emails until we're inside the office." Also, he went on, it was against company regulations for a senior executive to try to circumvent company policy by instructing a more junior executive to front his transportation costs. "Perry," Chester said softly, "you and I aren't even in the building yet, and you've already broken — what? — five or six standard company regulations!"

As the day went on, with one employee after another telling Perry one story after another about how corporate rules and regulations made it almost impossible to do their work, Perry looked more and more shattered. "I feel I don't know this company at all," he told Chester that night in the hotel bar. "I had no idea – none – how difficult it is to work for this organization."

That same night, Chester told me, he had a vision of his twenty-four-year-old self. That younger Chester was dressed in the same suit he wore when the company hired him out of business school. "I was looking at that person with disgust," Chester told me. He realized how complacent he had become about the lack of common sense in his company. He had simply found new ways to work around the rules rather than calling them out or advocating loudly for change. "The twenty-four-year-old me would have been kicking up a storm –" Chester said "– and the forty-one-year-old me then *did*."

Rules and regulations mattered, Chester knew that. It wasn't that he didn't respect them – it was that those rules and regulations had been somehow mutated and bastardized beyond the point of recognition. Beyond the point of ridiculousness, in fact. They no longer served anybody's best interests – "not the company's, the government's, not even the economy's." By protecting the organization, these rules and regulations had made company employees so myopic they had forgotten how to think straight.

Two months later, Chester had created a new department devoted to the restoration of common sense.

Change in organizations is difficult – and the more complex the industry, the harder it can be for any company to imagine and implement change. In this category, not surprisingly, is international banking.

For banks, public trust is paramount. Banks are responsible for our earnings, investments, retirement funds, and how we finance our day-to-day lives. Behind the scenes, banks are mandated to follow an intricate series of regulations around compliance and legal exposure. No wonder finance firms, more than other industries, often find themselves tied up in systems and processes, sometimes to the detriment of their customers and employees. That's why London-based Standard Chartered Bank—the first organization to get behind, and run with, the idea of creating an in-house Ministry of Common Sense—is such a bellwether in its industry, as is its founder, Gail Ursell.

When Gail set up the first-ever Ministry of Common Sense, her immediate focus was on company policies and procedures that ended up creating more confusion and annoyance than actual value. More than a corporate in-joke, the Ministry of Common Sense focused on solving *real* problems, untangling rules and procedures that seemed to have been written with no human being in mind. Ideas and submissions soon started pouring in. The first common-sense problem Gail's Ministry took on involved a code that all employees were asked to input on their travel forms. For no discernible reason, the code changed every few weeks, without warning. "Someone had been trying for four years to fix that," Gail recalls. "We got it done in six weeks."

At the same time, she knew she might make some people in the organization uncomfortable. She knew the Ministry could potentially ruffle a few feathers. Some people, she knew, might accuse her of disloyalty, of not acting in the bank's best interests, or of targeting various safeguards that *protected* the bank. But what was the alternative?

Six months after its founding, Standard Chartered Bank's Ministry of Common Sense had managed to solve a dozen or more common-sense problems in the company, from customer service to accounting. By any measure, the Ministry was a huge success, with the website receiving thousands of hits daily. More than just providing solutions, the Ministry also validated what employees were thinking and feeling. *Oh, I've had that problem too!* was one refrain. *I know exactly who can help with that.* For the first time in a long time, employees felt recognized not just as team members but as fellow humans. They learned it was perfectly okay to acknowledge that a regulation or procedure, one they had been following dutifully without complaint for years, made no sense. The Ministry communicated the message that there weren't two sets of rules after all, one for civilian life and the other for corporate life, and that employees had every right to expect common sense, empathy, and humanity in their workplace.

To Gail, the Ministry was more than just an informal fix-it lab. She hoped it would transform the corporate culture and send a message that the company would listen to any employee enterprising enough to come forward and ask for help. Over the next few months, more and more people did, and more and more companies began experimenting with the idea of setting up their *own* Ministries, with the following results:

> ➤ Before onboarding anyone, the company screened all applicants to show they had clean employment histories, even if there was no chance of the company offering them a job. Fair enough. Of course, this took time and resources. It also meant that applicants who *were* about to be offered jobs got caught up in this screening backlog, slowing down their onboarding and frustrating managers

who simply wanted to submit employment offers! The Ministry of Common Sense eliminated that provision.

> In another New York-based company, employees had twenty-four hours to submit their travel itineraries to a department manager for approval. Oftentimes managers didn't reply within that time period. After twenty-four hours, the online approval system reset, and the form was lost, which meant employees had to submit a new one. The Ministry created a new policy: managers could *veto* a travel itinerary, but failure to respond within twenty-four hours meant that requests were approved automatically.

> In one of the company's satellite offices in the southern United States, free coffee and snacks were available to all employees. But in an effort to save money, the company neglected to provide any soap or sponges to wash the dirty coffee cups. Allegedly some employees got sick. Most took twice-a-day coffee breaks at a nearby coffee shop. Two roundtrip coffee runs every day, times hundreds of employees, isn't exactly an advertisement for better productivity. The Ministry let all its employees know that the company would be providing soap and napkins that would a) reduce germs and sickness; and b) increase overall productivity. Soap and napkins appeared. Employees started drinking their coffee at work, and incidents of sickness went down.

So how do you set up a Ministry in your own company? The approach I use consists of three simple steps: Endorse (where you create a convincing case that senior management should endorse a Ministry); Energize (where you motivate the culture through a series of proof points that provide evidence that the Ministry works — and will continue to work); and Externalize (where by putting yourself in the shoes of others and seeing things through their point of view — customers,

> The top priority should be to reinstall common sense by saving money.

clients, employees in other departments — you reinstall common sense and empathy).

Go slowly. Everything I do happens during a 90-Day Intervention, creating short, meaningful initiatives to generate and maintain momentum while eliminating second-guessing (and politics) from the process.

ENDORSE

For a Ministry to succeed, you need to make it official. The Minister of Common Sense should be a full-time, salaried job, carried out and embraced with the approval of upper management. It can't be seen as a frivolous job. Often when employees are given a mandate, they don't take it. Do everything in your power to make sure this mandate *sticks*.

Before anything else, you need to address the short-term mindset of the CEO who, remember, has to justify his own role before a board or, if it's a listed company, shareholders. The best way inside the CEO's head is by emphasizing — you guessed it! — cost savings. No one has ever been fired for saving money. Endorse, Energize, and Externalize? The best Ministry initiatives tick all three boxes simultaneously. Common sense creates cost savings, improves the culture, and strengthens or refines customer experience.

That's why the best way to start is with what generates the biggest financial impact, so much so that one green light after the next starts flashing, ideally leading to a larger-scale version of the Ministry. That's why the top priority should be to *reinstall common sense by saving money.*

For example, when a small group of Toyota employees was asked to come up with a few clever ideas on how to save money, one team member asked a highly commonsensical question: "Does anyone know why we burn millions of dollars' worth of electricity in our production plants, plants staffed by robots that run 24/7, even when no humans are present?" Do robots need light? Well, if robots could talk, they would say no. No one at Toyota had ever considered this. Electricity costs were cut, and common sense prevailed.

A similar issue took place at a well-known hotel chain. I'm sure you've gone into a hotel bathroom to find a sign asking you to help save the environment by reusing your shower towel, and that if you want yours to be laundered, place it in the bathtub or in one corner of the room. Surprisingly, less than 15 percent of all hotel guests choose to "help save the environment." During a brainstorming session, a housekeeper came up with a brilliant idea. Instead of trying to appeal to customers' environmental awareness, she reframed the message differently: "Seven out of ten hotel guests choose to reuse their towels to help save our environment. Are you one of them?" This simple tweaking of words had a profound impact. A few months later, the housekeeping team had to change the number from "seven out of ten hotel guests" to "nine out of ten hotel guests." The planet felt the difference, and so did the hotel.

Common sense and cost savings? What could be better? That said, this happens only around 50 percent of the time. Once you go ahead with a project, make sure that whatever savings it generates will be divided fifty-fifty. Half goes to the department in question. The other half will be kept by the Ministry for its work and ongoing expansion.

The smartest part of this approach is that it neutralizes critics and naysayers. Every organization has a few. Okay, *a lot*. To get these people onboard, here's the secret carrot: you'll not only pay for the entire project, you'll also share 50 percent of any income generated from it with them. Whenever one of those quick 90-day initiatives succeeds, calculate the financial value, and use those funds to show other departments the benefits by example. Has anyone ever said no to receiving a check or objected to an initiative whose goal is *earning money?*

When CEOs and senior leadership become convinced that cost savings *and* common sense often work in tandem and that this Ministry thing really works, it's time to expand the Ministry's scope. Going forward, focus on common-sense issues that won't necessarily generate income, whether they involve employees, customers, or both. Some of these may indeed cost money. But you can use the funds generated through the cost-saving initiatives to make them become self-funding projects.

ENERGIZE

Once traction has been established among senior management, it's time to expand the reach of the Ministry to encompass the overall culture. Why culture? Because cost savings can only go so far in improving employee morale. If any and all suggestions employees come up with get stalled or bogged down, they will very soon get the impression that change, or even resistance to the status quo, is futile. The most important thing to import into an organization is *hope*. Hope shows up in proof points. Hope wears down skepticism. Hope is analogous to oxygen. The more improvements, the more hope, and the more oxygen will fill the hallways.

For example, in a global investment firm I worked for, one employee took aim against the company's regulation around computers. The rule was that the more senior a person was, the faster IT would fix his computer. Imagine the impact that being told you had to wait two weeks to get a new mouse had on morale. The employee's idea was to stock a vending machine with parts that were prone to wearing out or just plain not working—cords, mouses, adapters. Taking his cue from Apple's Genius Bar, he launched his own in-house canteen. It was first come, first served too.

Another example of employees taking initiative into their own hands came at Swiss International Air Lines. There, cabin crews had no mandate to handle onboard complaints. Instead, they had to fill out a report, which was then forwarded to a third-party complaint center to be handled. The cost per issue handled was $89—never mind the growing rage of the passenger who would wait months for an answer or resolution. The Ministry introduced a simple change in the guidelines, giving cabin crew members a mandate to handle passenger complaints when they occurred. Most cases (a spilled drink, etc.) could easily be handled for well under $89. This saved the company an enormous amount of money, generating both happier passengers *and* happier staff.

EXTERNALIZE

Once the culture has been elevated with hope, and oxygen, making its way through and helping employees see the world from other angles outside their own (thereby reinfusing empathy), it's time to take the ultimate step and focus on the people paying their salaries: the customers.

A few years ago, Microsoft was fielding hundreds of thousands of monthly calls it got from customers who'd bought Office products. Many believed that buying expensive software meant they were entitled to lifelong customer support. Microsoft saw things differently. The company made it difficult, if not impossible, to find the customer service phone number. Then a small group at Microsoft turned the problem upside down by coming up with a simple and brilliant solution. By cataloging all the calls, employees observed a few recurring patterns. There may have been hundreds of thousands of calls, but 80 percent or more of them were concentrated around fewer than one hundred issues. The team got to work, writing up each issue along with its solution.

Today, Office users who call Microsoft support call the company, identify the problem, and within seconds, a "paper" will arrive, addressing and solving 99 percent of all issues. The service is free. For anything more complex, for a fixed fee, they can continue the dialogue with an expert. Overnight, customers got their needs addressed. Microsoft started earning money—while also acquiring valuable data for the next Office update. A commonsensical solution.

BUT WHAT ABOUT REPORTING?

Ideally, you and the Ministry should report to the CEO, and absent that, to the COO or someone else at a similarly high level. Why? Because the Ministry needs to operate cross-functionally. The more independent your report is, the better chance you have of success.

To persuade your superiors to consider the Ministry approach, here's another idea: go underground. Try to identify a handful of cases that can be solved with a limited mandate. Remember in chapter 6 how meeting rooms gave an attendee ten minutes to confirm the meeting was underway, otherwise the room was reassigned? That actually happened, and one employee finally decided she'd had enough. After booking a meeting room, how many people, she wondered, do *not* show up? The system said it was 65 percent—yet her own analysis revealed that the number was closer to 5 percent. Why have a meeting confirmation function at all? It was eliminated. She kept swatting down one small daily irritation after the next, and before long people started coming up to her throughout the day for advice on solving similar issues.

Her portfolio of "issues solved" was exactly what she needed to build a solid case to create a Ministry—and her boss gave her the go-ahead to proceed in a more formal way. As her department hit the "silo" issue — certain nonsensical things couldn't be solved without engagement from other departments — her boss made the Ministry cross-functional, elevating her position to a CEO direct report.

But what happens if you encounter resistance? What if the CEO or CFO asks, *Why can't we just address these issues as they occur? Do we really need to set up an entire department?*

The answer is simple: attach an expiration date to the Ministry. If X number of issues isn't detected or solved within a six-month time period, you'll bag the whole idea. By managing expectations, you'll be measured against whatever goal you promise. You will quickly learn that the number of common-sense issues far exceeds anyone's expectations. Along the way, you'll reactivate the common sense of everyone around you, saving money, creating happier customers and, just as important, happier employees. Needless to say, all these things can easily be measured, valued, and celebrated.

Here are a few more commonly asked questions and answers.

Do I have to call it the "Ministry of Common Sense"?

No — you can call it whatever you want! But choose a name that stands out, gets attention, and is memorable and provocative.

What if the Ministry is slow to take off?

You can't expect a Ministry to be an overnight sensation. If you've already gone through my five-part program, my suggestion is to work backward. Use the problems your company has already uncovered and addressed as proof points. That way, instead of sitting at your desk merely waiting for other people to bring you this or that incoherent company-wide policy, you will already have a few success stories in the pipeline.

How should I deal with IT?

Don't hire a world-class IT team if you're setting up a Ministry website. Instead, consider installing a mailbox in a high-traffic location — outside your office, in the cafeteria, or by the coffee machine. Encourage everyone to fill out postcards with their issues. Compose a few lack-of-common-sense examples on a nearby poster as a prompt.

Should I market the Ministry?

Once you've secured buy-in for setting up a cross-functional Ministry, don't announce it on the first day. Work underground until you've established a few success stories. Trumpet things too loudly, and the skeptics will come out. So will some employees who believe a Ministry is tampering with things they should leave alone. In time, they'll find other weapons of resistance: *Nothing is happening with this thing. Look at how we're burning time and money. This is just a costly distraction.* And so on.

Going underground circumvents this. Once you have a couple of cases in hand, use them tactically. Ideally, they should serve to illustrate the real purpose of the Ministry. It's easier to convince others with real cases. You can also slowly reintroduce cases into the organization on a regular basis. As the Ministry gains traction, consider allying it with the company's communications department. Use its network to publicize positive stories that infuse hope throughout the organization.

Along the way, you'll learn a lot! Including what common sense is, and what it means in your company. This is where the commandments come into play.

Commandments? What commandments?

Glad you asked. Write down a list of ten to twelve guidelines to serve as the foundational principles of the Ministry. They can include things like "Let common sense prevail —ahead of red tape, ahead of silo separations, ahead of everything." And "In order of priority, common sense rules, followed by efficiency and cost savings." And "Common-sense issues are everywhere — and should be addressed and solved by anyone in the organization, no matter their status or function."

Who should run the Ministry?

The ideal candidate is passionate and energetic, with good social skills and a thorough knowledge of your industry. Think back to the 90-Day Intervention. Who there seemed the most excited about bringing about organizational change and has the fearlessness and perseverance to turn the Ministry into reality? The ideal candidate should be well-liked, well-respected, well-connected, and focused on making everyone in the company *work better.*

How should I get started?

The answer is *slowly and simply.* Ask staffers to vote for the most ridiculous or poorly thought-out policies or procedures in the workplace — the ones that drive everyone nuts.

Those, of course, would be the starting point for the Ministry and would empower the Minister to make significant changes. Once success is reached with those, other employees will be more eager to come forth with other corporate bottlenecks and roadblocks.

The Ministry should, of course, spend time with client-facing employees and teams from as many departments as possible. Instead of asking them, "What is stopping you from delivering what you want to deliver?" ask, "What are the biggest hurdles or impediments that keep you from delivering what customers want?"

What should I do first? The Ministry needs to deal with the bureaucratic problems that already exist—which is why the company should consider placing a three-month freeze on searching for new ones. Each company policy or procedure—or whatever obstacle is behind all the nonsense in the organization—should be examined closely. If it's a policy that refers to another policy, *both* policies should be studied and fixed. Ask yourself: What does this regulation achieve? What does it take away? If it takes away more than it achieves, get rid of it.

What's the connection with customers?

If you work in a customer-facing position, it's important to connect whatever problem you are trying to fix with your *clients*—and how a proposed change will affect *them*. Internal improvements should always lead to positive, improved customer experience.

You recommend using images in corporate settings—why?

In my experience, cartoons, and images in general, are a useful, nonthreatening way to highlight a lack of common sense in a company — whether they illustrate how hard it is to get a customer service representative on the line or the various machinations employees go through to get their expense accounts paid. Humor and informality also tend to dissolve the rise of corporate politics and make it less likely for employees to retreat into corporate mode.

Is there a failsafe way to come up with solutions?

As we discussed in chapter 8, my philosophy around creativity involves combining two ordinary things in a new way. The answers you're looking for can often be found by looking at your challenge from another angle. How would Amazon solve this problem? What would Google do? You might also consider using the "crowdfunding" path by tapping into the collective power of the minds of everyone in the organization. Write the challenge down and place it in a public setting — and see what comes of it.

How can a Ministry sustain its growth?

Once the Ministry starts to gain traction, you'll notice something remarkable. Volunteers will come forward. Employees will begin taking matters into their own hands, addressing and solving them. Some employees may prefer to be anonymous. Others will have no issue with using their names.

Are there any benchmarks for success?

To become an Eagle Scout in Boy Scouting, you first need to earn twenty-one merit badges. These patches prove you've attained proficiency in subjects ranging from Camping to First Aid to Personal Fitness to Emergency Preparedness.

When a Boy Scout shows off his achievements to his peers, it inspires *them* too.

If you've fixed, streamlined, or eliminated a common-sense problem, make sure you celebrate your victory, giving credit where credit is due. Consider creating actual rewards for jobs well done—badges, ribbons, or other totems of success, virtual or real. Whenever possible, positively link the change you've made to an existing KPI. At meetings, consider asking employees who submitted a stupid rule or regulation to be changed or eliminated to discuss its origins and also what made them realize it shouldn't exist.

Should I create a database?

One of the smartest things a Minister of Common Sense can do is create a list of the three to four individuals in the company who are good at fixing things or dealing with crisis. Once you've assembled the list, ask everyone on it for the names of five other people they would contact if *they* wanted to get something done. Often the same names will show up again and again. Bottom line? These people are doers and can be extremely useful if the Ministry comes up against any resistance.

How do I make sure that the Ministry stays on track?

Even a Ministry of Common Sense can lose its own direction with common sense by taking shortcuts, getting bogged down in too many compromises, or getting lazy and failing to take its own mandate seriously.

As the Ministry, how do you define common sense? Inscribe it on a plaque or write it down somewhere. Once or twice a year, revisit what you wrote. Make it a point to preserve what the Ministry stands for. And make sure your colleagues know the definition as well.

What if the Ministry is overwhelmed with issues?

Along with doing its job, the Ministry has an indirect goal of encouraging all employees to address challenges on their own. Naturally they're free to contact the Ministry at any time, but they should also feel empowered to question why certain procedures and processes are followed. In effect, unless the employees embrace the Ministry, it will be difficult to clean out the red tape and bureaucracy.

In fact, the goal should be thirty-seventy split. Thirty percent of all common-sense issues should be the province of the Ministry, and employees should be responsible for the other 70 percent. Rather than the Ministry of Common Sense shouldering all the responsibility for solving nonsensical issues within the corporate walls, common sense should become a company-wide mission.

What if employees are resistant to the Ministry?

Look, companies (and politics) being what they are, there will always be someone who feels attacked by the Ministry, who takes its very *existence* personally. It might be someone whose "policy" the Ministry just removed. Those people will always exist. Your weapon against them is communication — a steady torrent of success stories, small and large. Not only do these send a clear signal to the organization that common sense will prevail in the end, but these news nuggets will continue to inspire employees to take matters in their own hands. Who can kill an initiative everyone raves about that also saves money while creating happier employees and customers?

How can the Ministry make sure to address all of the issues?

The reality is, if you work in a big company, even having a Ministry of Common Sense won't ensure that everything goes according to plan or makes complete sense. If the Ministry is able to fix even a quarter of the problems in your organization, it's a success.

The sheer fact is that a Ministry trains employees to pay closer attention to what they do every day—to not just go through the motions. If employees see something that doesn't make sense to them, they should say something. If they don't, they're actually becoming a part of the problem.

Should the Ministry work toward planned obsolescence?

The Ministry of Common Sense has an additional mandate. A hidden one. An implicit one. In short, it should aspire to its own nonexistence or, at the very least, its own irrelevance. Put another way, it should cheerfully self-destruct when it no longer has any use to anyone in the company. Why would you need a Ministry to solve common-sense issues if common sense is so strongly embedded in the organization?

> The Ministry of Common Sense should aspire to its own nonexistence or, at the very least, its own irrelevance.

Before then, get to work. The goal is to have everyone in your company rediscover their own inner common sense, and act on it. To see the world through others' perspectives. To put yourself in other people's shoes, whether it's employees or customers. By restoring common sense, you'll also bring back empathy. When that happens, the Ministry can dissolve into day-to-day operations and go back to where it belongs. Park the customer-focus piece in the customer service department. Park the employee issues in HR. Distribute it across multiple divisions (though before you do this, write down those commandments again and have the person you give them to pledge to follow them).

More than anything else, the Ministry should serve to remind everyone that questions are meant to be asked, rules and regulations analyzed, procedures held up for inspection, and operations subject to reconsideration, up to and including the plastic packaging that imprisons the world's headsets! If these things only serve the company, its customers, and employees, they should stay. If they don't, they should go.

Why should what we do in business be different from what we do in life? How is *that* common sense? It's not.

May you and I always know the difference.

ONE MORE THING...

WHEN YOU WRITE A BOOK ABOUT THE lack of common sense, you not only begin noticing more and more examples of it in companies, you also become aware of your *own* daily moments of lunacy. How, for example, when you wait for the elevator, you press the UP button every few seconds, as if the elevator will somehow take note of how rushed you are and get there sooner. How at a traffic intersection, you repeatedly jab the WALK button, despite knowing that most of these buttons have been deactivated and exist only to give you and the other pedestrians the illusion of control. How when the TV remote doesn't work, we squeeze the volume or channel buttons harder, not realizing we need to change the batteries. How when you're hungry, you open the refrigerator door, scan the contents, close it delicately, and a minute later, open it again, scan the contents . . . and so on.

All of this is to say that a lot of the time, you and I lack just as much common sense in our own lives as companies do in theirs. Okay, maybe not *quite* that bad. I'm pretty sure I've only barely scratched the surface, actually. That's where you can help.

Now is your chance to vent, to tell all, anonymously or not, because we all deserve a good laugh, a good cry, or a good tantrum. I invite you to submit your best examples of corporate illogic, technological muddle-headedness, procedural missteps, and anything else that defies common sense to my website, MartinLindstrom.com/commonsense, or share them (and/or follow my daily updates) on:

@MartinLindstrom
Facebook.com/MartinLindstrom
LinkedIn.com/in/LindstromCompany
Instagram.com/LindstromCompany

Ideally, together we can launch a new common-sense movement, one where meetings begin and end on time, PowerPoints are a faraway memory, rules and regulations are minimal and actually have a point to them, empathy reigns . . . and opening a new pair of headphones doesn't require the skills of a Navy SEAL.

We're human. Isn't it time we all *acted* like it?

ACKNOWLEDGMENTS

On a frigid winter night two — or was it even three? — years ago, I made a dinner reservation for four people at Le Veau d'Or, a cozy, charmingly formal French restaurant on the Upper East Side of Manhattan, where the menu features dishes like leeks, snails, mussels, and *celeri remoulade*. My dinner companions that night were Jim Levine, my literary agent; Mark Fortier, book publicist extraordinaire; and Peter Smith, a writer I've worked with for more than a decade and, in my humble opinion, the best one can get. I'd spent all day preparing a long list of book concepts, and one after another I presented them to the group.

Nope. Doesn't work. It just doesn't excite me . . .

Finally, as I was sinking lower and lower into my seat, Jim asked the question that all writers should ask themselves before they begin a project: *What subject is closest to your passion?* Well, I was off and running. I roused myself and started babbling about the incomprehensible number of stupidities and inefficiencies I found myself facing in company after company, in country after country—"and then," I said, "this fantastic woman at a workshop came up with the term, 'Ministry of Common Sense' to address the inanities in her *own* organization, and . . ."

"There's your title," Jim said, and ten minutes later, as the snails started getting nostalgic for the warmth of their shells, the architecture of this book began taking shape, just like that.

That's why first and foremost I'd like to thank those three musketeers—Jim, Mark, and Peter—for their help with almost everything, from framing the book to selling it to helping to write and release it—basically giving birth to these pages. (The only thing they were not involved with was giving birth to me, but if they'd been in Denmark that day, I feel sure they would have fought over the forceps.) If one can talk about an A-team, it would be these three. Peter, thank you for connecting with my thinking, humor, and observations, and elevating all three to another level, a skill I can only envy you for having. Jim, thank you for believing in me continuously over the years—you're one of a kind. Thank you, Mark, for spreading the news and keeping up with the immense level of wishes and demands with which I bombard your *own* A-team.

Speaking of A-teams, I want to express my immense gratitude to my favorite editor, Rick Wolff, at Houghton Mifflin Harcourt, whose steady hand helped usher me out of the forest so I could better identify the trees. Iconic, thoughtful, and clear-thinking, Rick, in my opinion, is like one of those editors you see in movies, the kind that makes you think, *My*

God, I hope one day I get the chance to meet and maybe work with someone like that. It was my great fortune to be able to do just that. Thank you, Rick, for believing in this book, and in me.

With Rick comes the amazing team at Houghton Mifflin Harcourt. A special thank-you for going way beyond the call of duty goes to Laura Brady, senior director of manuscript editing, who worked miracles overseeing the copyediting and production of the book, and the equally tireless HMH publicist Marissa Page; Olivia Bartz, editorial associate, for her exhaustive efforts to review this manuscript and shepherd it from manuscript to finished book; and Rachael DeShano, for a wonderful copyedit. I also want to thank the entire HMH sales team, headed up by Ed Spade and Colleen Murphy, for its tremendous energy and enthusiasm in getting behind this book in a big, big way.

I can't thank the core team at Lindstrom Company enough for gathering content, reviewing pages, and working hard on the book's release. My gratitude goes to Rose Cameron, Cameron Smee, Signe Jonasson, Scott Osman, and Constantina Gogaki. Your help and support have been immeasurable.

Common sense is a genius dressed in everyday clothing — which can't help but make me think about Gail Ursell, head of governance and control in group human resources at Standard Chartered Bank. Gail, I'm forever grateful to you for coining the term "Ministry of Common Sense," your courage to push it through the organization while never losing hope, not to forget your incredible sense of humor. A special thanks to Bill Winters, CEO of Standard Chartered Bank, for our many inspiring conversations, your dedication to transforming the bank and creating an environment that allows people like Gail — and tens of thousands of employees across the world — to rediscover common sense. From the global leadership team to the many country heads, there are too many individuals at Standard Chartered Bank to thank individually, but please know how grateful I am and how much I value everyone there who has crossed my path.

Nor would this book exist without our wonderful clients who, in many cases, turned into close friends. Thank you for joining me on this journey into various aspects of corporate life, for sharing the vulnerable facets of your organizations, and for trusting that my unorthodox approach would end up yielding something beneficial. At the end of the day, belief amounts to only half the effort. Without belief — and hope — a culture won't exist, and a strong (and commonsensical) culture is what separates a successful company from a failure. I'd particularly like to highlight a couple of my clients, who are responsible for unique contributions to this book.

Thank you to Louisa Loran, who introduced me to Maersk and believed in me every step of the way. Louisa has an extraordinary ability to see complex issues in a clear, simple way and push things forward, through both front and back doors, making the entire organization appreciate, and believe in, the importance of culture. A special thank-you, too, to Catherina Kakko, global head of customer mindset at Maersk, who took the baton from Louisa and sprinted as fast as she could into the arms and sneaker soles of 88,000 Maersk employees. Cat, as everyone calls her, and her boss, Sonny Dahl, vice president and global head of customer experience and service at Maersk, are without a doubt two of the main reasons why Maersk can brag about a 200 percent improvement in its customer satisfaction scores today.

A very special thank-you, as well, goes to Mette Refshauge, Maersk's vice president of communications, who introduced another level of communication, one where "human-speak" runs the show, creativity is front and center, and communication isn't just for newsletters and corporate brochures but for Twitter, Instagram, Facebook, town halls, and GPS-equipped batons spinning across the globe.

I'd also like to give thanks to Maersk's Vincent Clark, chief commercial officer and senior vice president; CEO Søren Skou; and a handful of other amazing people who believed in the process, including Omar Shamsie (a remarkable human being who lives and breathes common sense), Mike Xue Gang Fang, Franck Dedenis, and Ulf Hahnemann, all of whom were among the first to jump out of the chicken cage and embrace my work. Having personally spoken to more than 5,000 people at Maersk, I apologize in advance to anyone who is *not* on this list! You are instrumental in making my work at Maersk happen. Thank you.

Another special thank-you goes to the Dorchester Collection—to Ana Brant, guest experience and innovation, who understood the importance of small data and the potential of its insights to improve hospitality long before anyone else did. Ana, you've been a remarkable source of inspiration to me and to the Dorchester Collection. Helen Smith, chief customer experience officer, not only contributed her valuable insight to this book but has also been instrumental in implementing common sense to the group—and for that I'm forever grateful. Nor am I overlooking the lifeblood of the organization, the general managers. Thank you especially to Edward Mady, U.S. regional director. I've said it before and want to stress it again: you, in my opinion, are the world's number one hotel general manager. I'd also like to thank Luca Virgilio, general manager at Hotel Eden in Rome, an individual who more than anyone I know truly "gets" (and lives) the concept of small data in hospitality; Zoe Jenkins, general manager at Coworth Park UK; and Franka Holtmann of Le Meurice in Paris. You are a remarkable group of amazing GMs.

My friends at Lowes, in particular Heather George, Brian George, and Tim Lowe — not to mention Brandon Green, vice president of host experience at Lowes Foods (and the man who invented the campfire concept); Kelly Davis, director of brand insights and strategy at Lowes Foods; Gary Watson, my favorite architect (Gary, what was your handicap again — two or twenty?) — all deserve a shout-out. I've referred to you here and there in this book for the simple reason that you have a very special spot in my heart.

Thanks to Melinda Paraie, CEO of Cath Kidston, and the rest of the Cath Kidston team for keeping up with my crazy thinking, and to the folks at Baring Capital for believing in my approach toward how best to transform businesses.

In the course of writing this book, I've also had extensive conversations with a ton of amazing people. In particular I'd like to thank Mickey Connolly, chairman at Conversant, for his fantastic support when it was most needed; my amazing friends Tiffany Foster and Frank Foster, managing director at Frontier Venture Capital; Lars Sandahl, CEO at Confederation of Danish Industry; and Tim Church, managing director and head of real estate, Australasia, at UBS; each of whom has set aside valuable time to offer solid input and criticism. Susanne Ruoff, former CEO of Swiss Post; Annette Mann, vice president of product management at Swiss

International Air Lines; Anders Fogh Rasmussen, CEO and founder of Rasmussen Global; Andre Lacroix, CEO of Intertek; Karin Sommer, head of marketing at Salling Group; Shelly Saxton; Nicole Fleiner at Brierley; Jim Motroni at Conversant; Eric Zaltas; Adrian Weiersmuller at Google; and Gary Tickle carved out time for interviews, reviewed the final manuscript, and shared stories, ideas, and comments. A special thanks to my former (no longer shivering) employee, Oliver Britz, who was there early in the creation of this book, some three years ago.

In addition, a fantastic group of people from Marshall Goldsmith's MG100 has also been instrumental in making this book a reality. First, of course, thanks to Marshall Goldsmith, who I met for the first time in 2018 when he invited me to join the MG100 club. Marshall: you quite literally introduced and redefined what coaching means in the world, and I couldn't be prouder that you agreed to write the foreword to this book. Another big thank-you goes to author and coach extraordinaire, Mark Thompson, for your ongoing inspiration and generosity; Laine Joelson Cohen with CITI; and author Dorie Clark for your great book-related input. There are so many amazing people in MG100 that I can only say, "I love you guys."

Finally, thank you to my readers, and I hope you get something from these pages. As Christopher Paolini once observed, "Because you can't argue with all the fools in the world, it's easier to let them have their way, then trick them when they're not paying attention."

May we all continue tricking them!

NOTES

Introduction

page

2 *A memo from the NFL:* Tim Daniels, "Report: NFL Bans Jersey Swaps, Postgame Interactions within 6 Feet amid COVID-19," July 9, 2020, https://bleacherreport.com/articles/2899474-nfl-bans-jersey-swaps-postgame-interactions-within-6-feet-amid-covid-19/.

8 Business Insider *recently named it:* Benjamin Zhang, "These Are the 10 Airlines You Want to Fly in Europe," *Business Insider,* August 13, 2018, https://www.businessinsider.com/best-airlines-in-europe-for-2018-ranked-according-to-skytrax-2018-8.

1. Why Won't My TV Turn On?

13 *TSA prohibiting the use:* "What Can I Bring?," Transportation Security Administration, https://www.tsa.gov/travel/security-screening/whatcanibring/all.

2. Where Has Empathy Gone?

27 *"Seeing things as they are":* Emma Ward, "Perceptive and Per-

sonal Quotes by Harriet Beecher Stowe," Literary Ladies Guide, September 23, 2017, https://www.literaryladiesguide.com/author-quotes/quotes-harriet-beecher-stowe/.

30 *In 2016, the Bureau of Labor Statistics:* Rana Foroohar, "We're Working Harder Than Ever, So Why is Productivity Plummeting?," *Time,* August 14, 2016, https://time.com/4464743/productivity-decline/.

37 *What goes through your mind:* Sam Wong, "The Feeling You Get When Nails Scratch a Blackboard Has a Name," *New Scientist,* February 28, 2017, https://www.newscientist.com/article/2123018-the-feeling-you-get-when-nails-scratch-a-blackboard-has-a-name/.

39 *According to the* New York Times: Pamela Paul, "From Students, Less Kindness for Strangers?," *New York Times,* June 25, 2010, https://www.nytimes.com/2011/09/30/opinion/brooks-the-limits-of-empathy.html.
According to a 2019 report: Niraj Chokshi, "Your Kids Think You're Addicted to Your Phone," *New York Times,* May 29, 2019, https://www.nytimes.com/2019/05/29/technology/cell-phone-usage.html.

40 *In another study from a few years ago:* Shalini Misra, Lulu Cheng, Jamie Genevie, and Miao Yuan, "The iPhone Effect: The Quality of In-Person Social Interactions in the Presence of Mobile Devices," *Environment and Behavior* 48, no. 2 (July 1, 2014): 275–298, https://journals.sagepub.com/doi/10.1177/0013916514539755.
"People who had conversations": Ibid.
Cogito, a Boston-based company: Kevin Roose, "A Machine May Not Take Your Job, but One Could Become Your Boss," *New York Times,* June 23, 2019, https://www.nytimes.com/2019/06/23/technology/artificial-intelligence-ai-workplace.html.

4. Politics: The Invisible Straitjacket

72 *In one, a munitions plant:* John Childress, "The Official and the 'Unofficial' Organization Chart," *John R. Childress' Disruptive Business Insights* (blog), March 26, 2017, https://blog.johnrchildress.com/2017/03/26/the-official-and-the-unofficial-organization-chart/.
The huge telecom company: Ibid.

74 *"You only find out":* Timestaff, "Swimming Naked When the Tide Goes Out," *Money,* April 2, 2009, http://money.com/money/2792510/swimming-naked-when-the-tide-goes-out/.

77 *"Model raindrops falling on a sidewalk":* Maya Kosoff, "41 of Google's Toughest Interview Questions," *Inc.,* January 26, 2016, https://www.inc.com/business-insider/google-hardest-interview-questions.html.

84 *A study done by anthropologists:* CD Lynn, "Hearth and Campfire Influences on Arterial Blood Pressure: Defraying the Costs of the Social Brain Through Fireside Relaxation," *Evolutionary Psychology* 12, no. 5 (November 11, 2014): 983–1003 U.S. National Library of Medicine, National Institutes of Health, https://www.ncbi.nlm.nih.gov/pubmed/25387270.

According to one source, campfires produce: Jon Staff, "Returning to the Campfire," *Thrive Global,* June 19, 2017, https://medium.com/thrive-global/the-science-behind-why-we-love-campfires-can-teach-us-a-valuable-lesson-about-modern-life-8e8d567ae5b.

5. You Have Been Denied Access to This Chapter

102 *Observing that everyone in his:* Tyler Wardis, "Busy Isn't Respectable Anymore," TylerwardIs.com (blog), https://www.tylerwardis.com/busy-isnt-respectable-anymore/.

103 *"a symptom of deficient vitality":* Forbes Quotes, "Thoughts on the Business of Life," *Forbes,* https://www.forbes.com/quotes/8129/.

108 *"do what you think is right":* Richard Milne, "Maersk CEO Søren Skou on Surviving a Cyber Attack," *Financial Times,* August 13, 2017, https://www.ft.com/content/785711bc-7c1b-11e7-9108-edda0bcbc928.

6. Show Me Your Deck!

124 *"Walk out of a meeting":* Catherine Clifford, "Elon Musk's 6 Productivity Rules, including Walk Out of Meetings that Waste Your Time," CNBC, April 18, 2018, https://www.cnbc.com/2018/04/18/elon-musks-productivity-rules-according-to-tesla-email.html.

7. What's That Lurking in the Shadows?

133 *Until 2012, Disney prohibited:* Nikelle Snader, "5 of the Worst Company Policies of All Time," *USA Today,* May 10, 2015, Cheat Sheet, https://www.usatoday.com/story/money/business/2015/05/10/cheat-sheet-worst-company-policies/70898858/.

Abercrombie & Fitch once issued: Sapna Maheshwari, "Exclusive: The Hairstyles Abercrombie has Deemed 'Unacceptable,'" *Buzzfeed News,* September 3, 2013, https://www.buzzfeednews.com/article/sapna/exclusive-abercrombie-hairstyle-rules-add-to-strict-look-pol#.budZErZmD3.

Under S. I. Newhouse: Bob Larkin, "30 Craziest Corporate Policies Employees Must Follow," Best Life, March 21, 2018, https://bestlifeonline.com/craziest-corporate-policies-employees-must-adhere-to/.

145 *The CEO, Steve DeFillippo:* Mark Johanson, "Why Do Some Companies Ban Certain Words?," BBC, August 31, 2017, https://www.bbc.com/worklife/article/20170830-why-do-some-companies-ban-certain-words.

Apple also prohibits the use: Sam Biddle, "How to Be a Genius: This Is Apple's Employee Training Manual," *Gizmodo,* August 28, 2012, https://gizmodo.com/how-to-be-a-genius-this-is-apples-secret-employee-trai-5938323.

At the Centers for Disease Control: VOA News, "Debate Continues on 'Banned Words' at CDC," *VOA News,* December 21, 2017, https://www.voanews.com/usa/debate-continues-banned-words-cdc.

147 *This is similar to one:* "Norwegian Alarm System Monitors Length of Office Lavatory Visits," *The Telegraph,* January 31, 2012, https://www.telegraph.co.uk/news/newstopics/howaboutthat/9051774/Norwegian-alarm-system-monitors-length-of-office-lavatory-visits.html.

8. Fear and Loathing in the Corporate World

151 *For example, a law is:* Chris Opfer, "10 Completely Archaic

Laws Still on the Books," October 29, 2012, HowStuffWorks.com, https://people.howstuffworks.com/10-archaic-laws-htm.

152 *In a 2014 TED Talk:* Amy Edmondson, "Building a Psychologically Safe Workplace," TedxHGSE, TedX Talks, uploaded May 4, 2014, YouTube video, 11:26, https://www.youtube.com/watch?v=LhoLuui9gX8.

153 *The* Harvard Business Review: Gary P. Pisano, "The Truth About Innovative Cultures," *Harvard Business Review,* January–February 2019, https://hbr.org/2019/01/the-hard-truth-about-innovative-cultures.

In 2012, the company launched: Charles Duhigg, "What Google Learned From Its Quest to Build the Perfect Team," *New York Times,* February 25, 2016, https://www.nytimes.com/2016/02/28/magazine/what-google-learned-from-its-quest-to-build-the-perfect-team.html.

As the New York Times *concluded:* Ibid.

9. So What Could the Answer Be?

174 *It's also perhaps a contributing factor:* Patricia Schaefer, "Why Small Businesses Fail: Top 7 Reasons for Startup Failure," Business Know-How, April 22, 2019, https://www.businessknowhow.com/startup/business-failure.htm.

INDEX

ABOUT THE AUTHOR

Martin Lindstrom is the founder and chairman of Lindstrom Company, the world's leading business and culture transformation group, operating across five continents and in more than thirty countries. The author of several *New York Times* bestsellers — his eight books have been translated into sixty languages — Lindstrom is among the "world's 100 most influential people" (*Time* magazine) and the "world's top 20 business thinkers" for 2020 (Thinkers50). You can follow Lindstrom and his team at LindstromCompany.com.